# Busting Gu
## *25 stupid gun arguments and how to refute them*

**BETSY F. YERGUNS**

**Busting Gun Nuts:**
**25 stupid gun arguments and how to refute them**

Copyright © 2016 by Betsy F. Yerguns
All rights reserved.

This book or any portion thereof may not be reproduced or used in any kind of manner at all whatsoever without the express written permission of the publisher, except for a few snarky bits on your blog. Of course, there's no point in writing this legal disclaimer, since criminals are just going to ignore it anyway. So fuck it; we may as well get rid of copyright laws altogether.

The author would like to thank a bunch of people who made this work possible, like that one person, and that other person (you know who you are), and also the guy who did that one thing. This research was funded by a generous grant from the Betsy Bloomberg Institute for Fuck Off NRA (FONRA), ~~and not by the FEMA shadow government at all~~.

# *Foreword to Second Edition*

Imagine if every state set its own requirements for obtaining a commercial drivers' license. Some states would have strict licensing regulations, and others would have few to none. The problem, of course, is that a whole lot of people would get a license in the state with the quickest/easiest/weakest requirements, and would then be legally allowed to drive in all 50 states.

Does that idea upset you? It should; it presents a clear threat to public safety.

That's what the NRA has in mind for guns. Concealed-carry reciprocity, also known as "Constitutional carry" or "the worst fucking idea ever," would effectively wipe out any gun permit regulations at the state level, and allow anyone to carry a concealed weapon anytime, anywhere. This dangerous agenda is at the very top of the NRA's wish list for a Trump administration; they sank over $30 million into his campaign, and they're going to expect what they paid for, the will of the people be damned.

Now more than ever, we need to stand up and fight. Loudly, angrily, and with naughty words.

The next four years will see a groundswell of Americans who repudiate everything Trump and his "good friends at the NRA" stand for: racism, xenophobia, misogyny and using deadly weapons to solve every problem. Gun proliferation MUST be recognized as part and parcel of those issues. The next four years should not be about asking for incremental change. They should be about branding gun proliferation as part of the same fucked up, oppressive shit sandwich as Trump's other policies, so that his gun laws will be undone along with everything else.

BETSY F. YERGUNS

The administration that takes over in 2020 will have a mandate to fix the damage wrought by Trump and the NRA, starting with bringing America's gun laws into step with the rest of the developed world.

# *Table of Contents*

*Introduction: "This is not the appropriate time to have this conversation." ........................................................ 1*

*Chapter 1: "Guns make you safer." ................................. 13*

*Chapter 2: What every other developed country has figured out .... 19*

*Chapter 3: "Knives, hammers, baseball bats, etc. ............. 27*

*Chapter 4: "Car accidents, falls, drownings, etc. ............. 31*

*Chapter 5: Crime and punishment .................................. 33*

*Chapter 6: Chicago ...................................................... 39*

*Chapter. 7: "Criminals don't follow laws!" .................... 45*

*Chapter. 8: Existing laws ............................................. 49*

*Chapter 9: The SECOND AMENDMENT!!!! ................. 53*

*Chapter 10: The Founding Fathers: fact and fiction ........ 57*

*Chapter 11: Two centuries of interpretation .................. 61*

*Chapter 12: The NRA - Before ..................................... 67*

*Chapter 13: The NRA today ......................................... 71*

*Chapter 14: But what about the RESEARCH?! ............. 77*

*Chapter 15: Gun-free zones! ......................................... 83*

*Chapter 16: "Hitler took the guns!" .............................. 87*

*Chapter 17: Muslims, mental illness, and other misdirections ......... 91*

*Chapter 18: "Most gun owners are law-abiding" ...until they're not ........................................................ 93*

*Chapter 19: "There's nothing we can do." ..................... 95*

INTRODUCTION

# "This is not the appropriate time to have this conversation."

We hear this every time: after the horrific mass shooting at Columbine High School. After the 2007 slaughter at Virginia Tech. After the Fort Hood shootings in 2009, and again in 2014. After Aurora. After Newtown. Isla Vista. Oregon. San Bernardino. Orlando. Countless others that didn't make headlines, but left a devastating wake of grief, rage and loss.

The gun lobby and conservative pundits immediately shut down any attempt to talk about meaningful gun legislation that would save lives. They even take the moral high ground: "How dare you try to politicize this tragedy? You can't even let the families grieve without pushing your agenda!"

So when exactly would be a good time to talk about how to stop this? Because if we're supposed to wait for a day when there aren't any shootings, it's <u>never going to happen</u>.

We talked about terrorism prevention immediately after 9/11, and put countless new safeguards in place. We improve fire prevention methods and alarm systems after a fire. We require manufacturers to make their products as safe as possible - autos, toys, baby equipment, pharmaceuticals - in an effort to save lives. After any tragedy, it's our moral and ethical and legal responsibility to do everything we can to prevent it from happening again.

You know what really disrespects the dead? Refusing to address a problem that has killed more Americans in the last 58 years than <u>all the U.S. wars since the Revolution</u>. We want fewer tragedies. We want less grieving. And we want no more moments of silence.

That's not what the Founding Fathers intended, and it's not something we can live with anymore.

We've all been too quiet for too long. If not now, when?

**How to use this book**

If you've already given enough of a shit about gun violence to peruse this book in the first place, you are helping us to move toward a solution. The more people are educated about the cold, hard facts of gun violence, the more progress we make. It's already happening, and you get to be a part of it.

Think of this book as your all-in-one reference manual and arsenal against the brain-killingly dumb arguments you encounter from gun nuts on social media, at family dinners, in stores and businesses, on the news, at monster truck pulls, or wherever you happen to encounter them. You don't *have* to argue with them (though it's fun) - you can just as easily use this book to learn about the history of America's gun-rights and gun-control movements (SPOILER: They're not as opposed as you may think). The chapters are designed to be read in any order, so feel free to skip to the ones you're most interested in first.

You're not likely to change the mind of anyone in the From-My-Cold-Dead-Hands camp, anyway. But the other 90% of Americans who think we need stronger gun laws now might just hear your voice, listen to evidence, and be inspired to speak up too. And join the growing movement to restore America's gun laws to their former sanity.

Disclaimer: This book contains a fuckton of swearing and shitty attitude. This is a deliberate narrative choice on the author's part: if someone's more upset by bad words than by a classroom of first-graders getting blown away by a maniac with an AR-15, they are the problem. Gene here is a good example:

Gene    And on and on and on with no agreement or real answer except, I keep mine civil with no foul language
Like · Reply · 41 mins

Civility ended for many of us at Sandy Hook
Like · Reply · 8 mins

**Betsy F. Yerguns** If by "civil" you mean "continuing to root for an organization that authors racist SYG laws and gets rich off the blood of children, urging inaction in the face of a crisis that kills 30,000 Americans every year," well then you, sir, are indeed one civil motherfucker.
Like · Reply · Just now

Gunhumpers often insist they only want a calm, reasoned, factual debate, right up until they threaten to shoot you. If you challenge them – which you should – you'll probably be met with lots of scary noises and threats. Sometimes they'll even threaten your family too, to show what law-abiding Good Guys they are and why they should be trusted to carry deadly weapons everywhere.

**Marvin**
you need to keep that gag in your mouth. if you don't, I don't know if your going to live.

**Marvin**
if you don't keep your mouth shut you are going to loose your family.

**Betsy F. Yerguns**
I'm actually part of a team conducting research on what percentage of gun nuts are tiny-dicked cowards. So far it's 100%. Thank your for your participation.

## Shit gunhumpers say: six quickies to get you started

*If we ban guns……*

Stop. Stop right there. No organization or lobby is calling for a total ban on guns. I don't care what the NRA or Fox News or your cousin Jerry told you. There is not and has never been a serious reform effort that seeks to ban guns altogether. If someone insists otherwise, they're either lying, have been lied to, or have mistaken *Red Dawn* for a documentary. The gun safety movement includes millions of law-abiding gun owners who are sickened by our culture of shoot-first insanity. Yes, there are some individuals who want guns banned, but frankly this a) just plain not going to happen, and b) does not drive policy.

---

**Fun Fact! If you support even one of these, then congratulations – you support gun control!**

Background checks for all sales and transfers (no exceptions)

Stricter penalties for illegal trafficking / providing a gun to a prohibited person

Requiring guns to carry titles and insurance

Limits and/or taxes on ammunition

Mandatory licensing and training, renewed every 1-2 years

Psychological screening for gun permits

Repealing open carry

Repealing concealed carry

Repealing federal prohibitions on gun violence research and civil liability for gun manufacturers

Banning assault weapons and armor-piercing bullets

Revoking the NRA's tax-exempt status

"Gun control" means many things to many people, but one thing it does NOT mean is prohibiting private ownership of firearms. This is a) impossible, unless you are North Korea, and b) a scare tactic used by the NRA to convince the gullible that the Boogeyman is "coming for your guns."

No matter what position you hold on any issue, it's very important to frame your arguments assertively rather than defensively. "We don't want to ban guns!" is a bad way to start, since right away it puts you in a position of weakness AND helps legitimize your opponent's accusation by repeating it. Instead, we're making what we DO want loud and clear:

We want sane, enforceable gun laws. We want <u>loophole-free background checks,</u> <u>state licensing of gun dealers</u>, mandatory training, licenses and permits for all gun owners, renewed as regularly as a driver's license. We want guns to have titles and carry insurance, like cars. We want to keep guns out of the hands of convicted felons, domestic abusers, and <u>people who are a danger to themselves or others</u>—including people who have a tendency to brandish a gun every time there's an argument or conflict.

*In the eyes of our justice system, this dickhead is a heroic citizen*

We want better mental health care and screening, but we also want to <u>cut through the bullshit</u> of blaming America's gun problem solely on mental illness. Every country on earth has mental illness, and domestic abuse, and nasty custody battles, and poverty, and road rage, and violent entertainment. Know what they don't have? Guns everywhere within easy reach at all times, turning what should have been an argument or fistfight into a gunfight, or an unsuccessful suicide attempt into a successful one.

==Guns don't kill people – people kill people.==

This is like saying, "Cars don't kill people – drunk driving kills people." Which, strictly speaking, is true. It's also a condescending dodge. We're all pretty clear on the fact that cars and guns and other machines do not operate themselves. Our concern is about the people operating them.

> **Jason**  Please don't be so naive....guns don't kill people, people kill people. Example, IEDs. I'd much rather dodge bullets occasionally then have to worry any sec while driving that I'm going to explode. Guns don't work in Iraq against our military, but IE... See more
> Like · Reply · 👍 3 · 3 hrs
>
> **Betsy F. Yerguns** ==People kill people with guns. People who should not have guns kill people who should be able to walk around freely== in society without encountering a heavily armed terrorist with guns that they should never have been allowed to have in the first place. But that's hard to fit on a bumper sticker, so that might excuse your ignorance.
> Like · Reply · Just now · Edited

Imagine doing fucking NOTHING about drunk driving - each state setting a different drinking age, and some even passing laws making it *easier* to drink and drive. That's what we used to have.

In 1980, alcohol-related traffic deaths were the number-one killer of Americans between the ages of 15 and 24. "Drunk driving seemed like the only socially acceptable form of homicide in this country," says Candace Lightner, founder of Mothers Against Drunk Driving. "The attitude toward perpetrators was benign, if not passive."

There were even those who thought alcohol and driving went together just fine, that no one had a right to make their decisions for them, and so on. People actually wrote letters to newspapers insisting that they could drive just fine while drunk; it was no big deal. Others accused reformists of wanting to ban alcohol and usher in a dystopian nanny state. Some suggested getting rid of the minimum drinking age altogether, in order to make roadways "safer."

LONG ISLAND OPINION

## LONG ISLAND OPINION; DRINKING AND DRIVING CAN MIX

By PHILIP B. LINKERPhilip B. Linker of Bayport is an associate professor of English at Suffolk Community College.
Published: June 3, 1984

LAST Saturday night I drove home drunk or almost certainly that would have been the indication from any breath or blood test that I might have been required to take. I drove home drunk the Saturday before that, too, and the one before that, and the one before that, in what probably amounts to a fairly consistent pattern over the last 25 years, ever since I have been licensed to drive.

Everyone else got so fucking fed up with this bullshit killing their loved ones by the tens of thousands that they started a grassroots movement. They lobbied legislatures in every state to form task forces on drunk driving. They worked to pass state and local laws to strengthen the penalties for driving drunk, AND for providing alcohol to people who shouldn't have it. They ran public-awareness campaigns that educated people about the dangers of drunk driving, and pushed to create a system that kept track of repeat offenders.

Automobile makers got with this new program, designing safety features that prevented impaired driving and minimized injuries during accidents. Alcohol distributors promoted awareness by urging consumers to "drink responsibly." People and businesses that knowingly provided alcohol to the wrong people were held legally accountable for their actions.

And we did it all without banning cars OR alcohol! Instead we studied the problem from many angles, using that research as the basis for laws regulating blood alcohol content, sentencing, educational programs and more. Ultimately, awareness + laws + safety technology = changed cultural attitudes about drinking and driving. Look at how fucking horrifying that letter to the editor is (above). We recoil in astonishment from the writer's calm – one might even say smug – assertions that everyone is making a big deal out of nothing. "Twenty-five thousand killed by drunk drivers every year? Who fucking cares - I can hold *my* liquor!"

> *"You kick a few pebbles, you turn a few stones, and eventually you have an avalanche."*
>
> – Candace Lightner

Drunk driving still happens, of course. People are people, and a few will always disregard these regulations. And when they do, they face legal consequences that impact their businesses, bank accounts, families and lives. Since the grassroots effort against it began more than thirty years ago, we've reduced the number of drunk driving deaths by 50%.

This is what we're doing now with gun violence.

*You're a hoplophobe!*

"Hoplophobia" is a term invented by doomsday prepper Jeff Cooper in 1962 to describe "an irrational fear of weapons or armed citizens." It does not appear in any edition of the Diagnostic and Statistical Manual of Mental Disorders, because it is entirely made up and does not exist.

Maybe if you started hyperventilating while you were in a museum looking at a 16th century Wheelock pistol in a glass case, that *might* fit the diagnosis. But there's nothing irrational about fearing weapons – especially weapons wielded by dangerous and/or unstable people – that are used in more than 10,000 murders each and every year.

*You're so ignorant about guns that you don't even know the difference between a TKB-517 and a .4576927 Elephant Shredder."*

> *"Suppose that a 100-person firing squad was about to execute an innocent person.... They hand you a rifle and offer to let you shoot with them. Taking the shot or walking way makes no difference— the innocent person will die either way. From a moral point of view, however, you should not join in."*
>
> – Ethicist Jason Brennan

So I can't want laws against drunk driving because I don't know how to fix a carburetor or take apart an engine block? I can't name every model in the Ford F-series produced between 1967-1972, so I need to shut up about automobile safety and regulations?

This is a distraction intended to place the gun worshipper in a position of superior power and knowledge, and it is meaningless bullshit. I don't give a fuck about the details of what kind of weapons the next mass shooter uses. I'm more interested in how to stop him.

*I carry a gun in case I have to defuse a situation.*

Pro tip: No human being has ever, in the history of ever, been "calmed down" at the sight of a deadly weapon. I wouldn't be. You wouldn't be. People pull out guns during conflicts for one reason: to compel respect and fear. It's a way of saying, "I hold the power in this situation. Respect my authority or I will kill you." This is called the weapons effect – when the only tool you have is a hammer, every problem looks like a nail.

> *I left my gun sitting on my porch and it didn't get up and shoot anyone by itself!*

You left a loaded weapon sitting unattended? Wow, you must be one of those responsible gun owners I hear so much about. The NRA wants you so crazy-paranoid that you think you need to walk around armed at all times. You don't look like a Good Guy. You look like a fucking coward.

These are some of the things people say, even as they accuse you of ignoring "facts" in favor of your own irrational emotions. Fuck that. You want to talk facts? Then stop blocking federal research on gun violence and swallowing the NRA's fear jizz.

As you may have noticed, positive framing doesn't have to be the same thing as being polite. Fuck polite. These are people who mock the deaths of children, who publicly brandish weapons in an (unsuccessful) effort to intimidate those who disagree with them. They have mapped out a nightmare agenda to make guns more and more available to more and more people, insisting even as the body count climbs to five digits that their killing machines are making us *safer*. For decades they've gotten away with bullying anyone who dared to stand up to them, until fewer and fewer of us did.

That's why I'm a Betsy. That's why I wrote this book. The overwhelming majority of Americans want better gun control, and a small but powerfully vocal minority holds the rest of the country hostage to its paranoid fear and greed. The time for calm, respectful compromise is fifty years in the past. We lose between 88 and 91 people to gun violence every day, and we are motherfucking sick and tired of it. We won't stop until we've done everything we can to save as many lives as possible.

We're not the silent majority any longer.

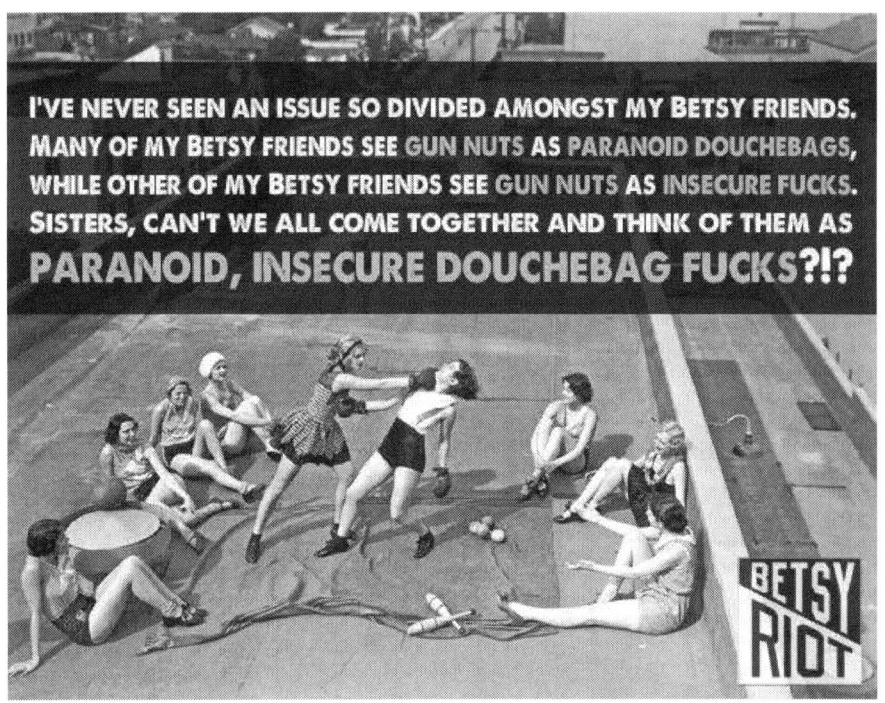

CHAPTER 1

## *"Guns make you safer."*

If this were true, the U.S. would be the safest nation on earth. We have more guns than any other country in the world (estimated at around 300 million), and *over 20 times* the rate of firearm deaths per capita of any other high-income nation.

A 2016 Harvard Injury Control Research Center firearms research summary found that "Per capita U.S. gun deaths vastly exceed all other high-income countries," and concluded that "It is virtually impossible to see these data and still claim that guns in the U.S. promote safety rather than death."

A 2016 National Institutes of Health study concluded that "The United States has an enormous firearm problem compared with other high-income countries, with higher rates of homicide and firearm-related suicide. Compared with 2003 estimates, the [2010] US firearm death rate remains unchanged while firearm death rates in other countries decreased."

> You may hear arguments that it's not fair to compare only high-income nations. But this is standard practice in all global health research, and the best way to control for other factors that affect countries' rates of gun violence (such as armed military conflicts).
>
> Also, "We're not THE deadliest nation in the world!" is a pretty shitty defense.

In 2013 (the most recent year for which complete data are available from the Centers for Disease Control and Prevention) there were 33,636 fatal shootings in the United States, grouped into three categories:

> *"The solution to gun violence is more guns!"*
>
> Kind of like the solution to drunk driving is more alcohol, the solution to lung cancer is more cigarettes, and the solution to fire is gasoline? All <u>credible research</u> shows that more guns lead to more violence.

## Homicides

The 11,208 homicides committed with firearms accounted for *over two thirds* (70%) of all homicides that year. That's 3.5 gun homicides per 100,000 people – by far the highest in the industrialized world.

For many people, "gun homicide" conjures images of Bad Guys in ski masks robbing banks, or shootouts with police. But, just as we've had to rethink our ideas of sexual assault, we also need to expand our understanding of gun violence. It's a mistake to think of either solely in terms of random attack by faceless strangers. Of the cases where the relationship between the victim(s) and perpetrator(s) are known, more than three-fourths are committed by someone known to the victim, and they may even have a close relationship. A lot of shootings happen in the heat of the moment – road rage, domestic violence, arguments that turn deadly.

> Gun nuts are fond of using FBI statistics to argue that shovels or tennis rackets or rubber chickens are used as murder weapons more often than specific types of guns. ("Knives kill more people than rifles!") Such claims always omit stats on handguns – the <u>most popular choice of weapon</u> in premeditated crime homicide, robbery and sexual assault.

### Domestic violence

The presence of a gun in the home is <u>far more likely</u> to result in a violent death for someone living there:

- In 55% of cases where women age 15-50 were killed by an intimate partner in 2005, the perpetrator didn't choose a knife, a hammer, a bowling ball or a swimming pool – they chose a gun. Family and intimate assaults with firearms are 12 times more likely to result in death than non-firearm assaults.

- The presence of a gun in the home is associated with a 3-fold increased homicide risk within the home. This risk is eight times higher when the offender is an intimate partner or relative of the victim, and *20 times higher* when previous domestic violence exists.

- A study of women physically abused by current or former intimate partners revealed a 5-fold increased risk of homicide when the partner owned a firearm.

Laws that keep guns out of the hands of domestic abusers will result in fewer lethal family and intimate assaults.

### *Suicides:*

*"If people want to kill themselves, they'll find a way to do it no matter what!"* True, if they're determined. But most aren't - the vast majority of suicides are impulsive and unplanned. The CDC classifies "easy access to lethal methods" among suicide risk factors. When there's a gun at the ready, the likelihood of suicide not only goes up, but so do the chances that the attempt will be lethal. (In fact, a surprising number of suicides take place at gun ranges.)

Of the 41,149 people who took their own lives in 2013, slightly more than half (21,175) did so with a gun that, in many cases, was improperly stored or secured. That's 6.7 gun suicides per 100,000 people... again, the highest in the world. It's not hard to see why guns are the number-one weapon of choice in both homicides and suicides. They're quick,

> "But suicides don't count!" Really? Why don't they? They're deaths caused by guns. The victims are just as dead, their families and communities just as devastated. Does it matter who pulled the trigger?

have a high rate of success (96.5%, compared to a 67% success rate for attempts involving poison or cutting), and are readily available everywhere. EVERYWHERE – even places that tightly restrict the sale and distribution of other things.

There's a reason we put suicide barriers on bridges – and they do work. Do they work 100% of the time? No, but they still save lives. Restricting easy access to firearms directly correlates with a drop in impulsive (usually teen) suicides. When the Israeli Defense Forces instituted a policy in 2006 that prohibited soldiers from taking their guns home with them on weekends, adolescent suicides plummeted by 40%.

> I thought of my friend John, a husband and father, who was depressed about school and couldn't buy beer in Utah because it was Sunday, so he bought a gun and shot himself.

## *"Accidents"*

"Unintentional firearm deaths" make up 1% of gun deaths annually. Approximately every other day in America, a child shoots and kills themselves or someone else with a loaded, unsecured gun. This is usually called an "accident" rather than what it is: criminal negligence. Usually the (ir)responsible gun owner faces no charges because "they've suffered enough." As of 2014, 28 states and Washington, D.C. had some kind of child access prevention (CAP) laws on the books...meaning that 22 had none at all. Not shockingly, states with safe storage laws have lower rates of child mortality due to firearms. [See also: smart guns]

Then there are "accidental discharges" (or "whoopsies"). The Good Guys have an awful lot of whoopsies in parking lots, churches, legislative offices, courthouses, stores, coffee shops, at graduation, at work, at gun ranges, in cars, in their own homes, and especially, it seems, in public restrooms. Or they are forgetful-heads who leave their loaded, unsecured weapons where the Toddler Militia and/or Bad Guys can find them.

Unlike every branch of the U.S. military, civilian law enforcement does not automatically equate "unintentional" discharge with "negligent." Each state, city and municipality can set its own ordinances regarding a whoopsie. These often conflict with each other and are enforced inconsistently, if at all.

> If lives aren't enough to persuade someone to give a shit, maybe they'll care about gun violence costing U.S. taxpayers approximately $229 billion each year. That's billion, with a B.

Finally, each year 70,000 non-fatal firearm injuries are brushed aside as trivial, or at least not as meaningful as deaths. Never mind the physical, emotional and financial damage inflicted on victims and their families can cause a lifetime of trauma for victims, their families and communities.

Gun violence is the one area where, if you survive, you literally don't count.

CHAPTER 2

# *What every other developed country has figured out*

The U.S. has the world's highest rate of gun ownership, with 88 guns for every 100 people. That's more than Yemen, for crying out loud.

It's important not to misinterpret this as, "88 out of every 100 Americans owns a gun." The number of gun-owning households has actually declined to 1 in 3. What this means is that the people who DO own guns now own an average of 8 of them, and are becoming increasingly radicalized.

Contrary to the oft-repeated refrain, Canada does not have more firearms than the U.S. (9.9 million to our 300 million), nor a higher rate of gun ownership (30.8 firearms per 100 people, compared to our 88/100).

Israel has 7.3 guns per 100 people – again, all registered in a database. All Israeli citizens, male and female, are conscripted into the military at age 18 and receive extensive mental health screening and training in how to use (and NOT use) firearms.

Switzerland, the gunhumpers' imagined utopia, has plenty of gun control laws - including a national firearms registry.

North Korea is the only country on earth that completely bans all gun ownership by civilians. And to be clear, no U.S. political party, lobby, or regulation movement thinks an oppressive totalitarian regime is a good model to follow.

But the facts are clear: countries that strictly regulate access to firearms have significantly lower rates of gun-related homicide and suicide.

Popular comparison countries include the U.K. Australia, Japan, Norway and ......... wait, Honduras?

**HUH???**

The regulation of guns in Honduras is actually categorized as "permissive," and gun ownership is not mandatory in Switzerland (or anywhere, except Nucla, Colorado, U.S.A.).

Let's take a look at these countries: all of them have mental illness, poverty, secularism, violent movies and video games (the favorite scapegoats of anti-regulation arguments) at rates relatively comparable to our own. What they don't have is easy access to guns, anywhere, anytime, by anyone.

But they *do* have them. Many (in fact most) countries restrict specific types of weapons – automatic, semiautomatic, and pump-action shotguns. Even restrictive governments like China, Indonesia, Iran and

Vietnam allow guns for hunting and sport shooting, though these are subject to very strict licensing requirements, with severe penalties for illegal possession and trafficking that range from prison to execution.

Among high-income nations, the U.S. leads the world – and not in a good way:

Grinshteyn and Hemenway   Violent Death

**Table 4** Total Death Rates per 100,000 Population by Non-US High-Income Countries, 2010

| Country | Firearm Homicide Rate | Non-Firearm Homicide Rate | Total Homicide Rate | Firearm Suicide Rate | Non-Firearm Suicide Rate | Total Suicide Rate | Unintentional Firearm Death Rate | Undetermined Firearm Death Rate | Total Firearm Death Rate |
|---|---|---|---|---|---|---|---|---|---|
| Australia | 0.2 | 0.9 | 1.1 | 0.8 | 10.2 | 11.0 | 0.0 | 0.1 | 1.0 |
| Austria | 0.2 | 0.4 | 0.5 | 2.7 | 12.4 | 15.1 | 0.0 | 0.1 | 3.0 |
| Belgium | 0.3 | 0.7 | 1.1 | 1.3 | 17.1 | 18.4 | 0.0 | 0.1 | 1.8 |
| Canada | 0.5 | 1.0 | 1.5 | 1.7 | 9.9 | 11.6 | 0.0 | 0.0 | 2.3 |
| Czech Republic | 0.1 | 2.4 | 2.6 | 1.4 | 11.2 | 12.5 | 0.1 | 0.2 | 1.8 |
| Denmark | 0.2 | 0.6 | 0.8 | 1.3 | 8.8 | 10.1 | 0.0 | 0.0 | 1.6 |
| Finland | 0.3 | 1.6 | 1.9 | 3.3 | 14.5 | 17.8 | 0.0 | 0.0 | 3.6 |
| France | 0.2 | 0.4 | 0.6 | 2.2 | 14.3 | 16.5 | 0.1 | 0.3 | 2.8 |
| Germany | 0.1 | 0.5 | 0.6 | 0.9 | 11.3 | 12.3 | 0.0 | 0.1 | 1.1 |
| Hungary | 0.1 | 1.4 | 1.5 | 0.8 | 24.1 | 24.9 | 0.0 | 0.0 | 0.9 |
| Ireland | 0.4 | 0.5 | 0.8 | 0.5 | 10.1 | 10.7 | 0.0 | 0.1 | 1.0 |
| Italy | 0.3 | 0.4 | 0.8 | 0.9 | 5.7 | 6.6 | 0.1 | 0.0 | 1.3 |
| Japan | 0.0 | 0.3 | 0.3 | 0.0 | 23.1 | 23.1 | 0.0 | 0.0 | 0.0 |
| Netherlands | 0.2 | 0.7 | 0.9 | 0.2 | 9.4 | 9.7 | 0.0 | 0.0 | 0.5 |
| New Zealand | 0.2 | 1.1 | 1.2 | 1.0 | 11.3 | 12.3 | 0.0 | 0.0 | 1.2 |
| Norway | 0.0 | 0.6 | 0.7 | 1.7 | 9.5 | 11.2 | 0.0 | 0.0 | 1.8 |
| Portugal | 0.5 | 0.5 | 1.0 | 1.1 | 9.3 | 10.4 | 0.0 | 0.2 | 1.8 |
| Republic of Korea | 0.0 | 1.3 | 1.3 | 0.0 | 31.5 | 31.5 | 0.0 | 0.0 | 0.0 |
| Slovakia | 0.2 | 1.0 | 1.2 | 0.9 | 10.8 | 11.7 | 0.4 | 0.2 | 1.8 |
| Spain | 0.1 | 0.6 | 0.7 | 0.4 | 6.4 | 6.9 | 0.1 | 0.0 | 0.6 |
| Sweden | 0.2 | 0.7 | 0.9 | 1.2 | 11.0 | 12.2 | 0.1 | 0.0 | 1.5 |
| United Kingdom | 0.0 | 0.3 | 0.3 | 0.2 | 6.6 | 6.8 | 0.0 | 0.0 | 0.2 |
| United States | 3.6 | 1.7 | 5.3 | 6.3 | 6.1 | 12.4 | 0.2 | 0.1 | 10.2 |

*Australia*

In 1996, two things significantly changed Australia's gun laws: on April 28-29, a lone gunman killed 35 people and injured 23 others with an arsenal of weapons and ammunition, including an AR-15. Immediately Prime Minister John Howard introduced the National Firearms Programme Implementation Act 1996, which quickly passed with strong bipartisan support even from states and territories that had previously opposed gun control measures. The new regulations included:

- restricted ownership of high-capacity semi-automatic rifles and shotguns and pump-action shotguns;

- required universal firearms licensing in which the serial number of each firearm is registered to the owner;
- strictly enforced penalties for selling guns to "prohibited persons"
- a federal gun buyback program, which removed 650,000 guns from circulation (<u>1/5 of the total stock</u> of firearms) and reduced the number of gun-owning households by 50%.

Anti-regulation folks try to claim that the buyback program led to an increase in violent crime, which is <u>a pretty weak lie</u>. <u>All evidence</u>, in fact, shows the opposite: within the next decade, firearm homicides fell 47%, and firearm suicides by <u>an astonishing 80%</u>.

Australia has had exactly <u>zero mass shootings</u> since 1996. Today no more than 20% of all homicides in Australia are committed with a gun, compared to 63-70% in the U.S.

*The U.K.*

As always, anti-regulation extremists clamor that the U.K. is a gunless nightmare hellscape of violent crime. Let's check out the state of guns in each of the U.K.'s four constituent countries to see if this is true (HINT: it isn't):

England and Wales: 6.2 firearms per 100 people, total of <u>4 gun homicides and 78 gun suicides</u> in 2012.

Scotland: 5.5 firearms per 100 people, total of <u>2 gun homicides and 12 gun suicides</u> in 2012.

Most regular beat police in these countries do not carry guns – a policy supported by the <u>overwhelming majority</u> of the Police Federation. Why? Because an armed populace makes their jobs more difficult and dangerous.

BUT: Every police force has a specially-trained firearms unit. When the use of deadly force is deemed necessary "to stop an imminent threat to life," specially-trained firearms officers are dispatched.

Northern Ireland is the exception, with 21.9 guns per 100 people, total of 4 gun homicides and 4 gun suicides in 2011. Thanks to the Belfast Agreement, it's not subject to the same strict civil firearms regulations as the rest of the U.K., and all its police officers are armed. (Northern Ireland alone accounts for why the U.K. is one of the top importers of guns.)

*Japan*

Home to some of the strictest gun laws in the world, Japan has the lowest number of firearms….and, by an amazing coincidence, one of the lowest rates of gun violence. What's encouraging is that Japan previously had fairly high rates of both gun ownership and violent crime, but they were able to virtually eliminate one by clamping down on the other.

Civilians are not permitted to own handguns, and must pass rigorous licensing requirements to own air rifles or shotguns. Without a firearm license, even holding a gun in your hand is a crime. To get a license, each applicant must:

- pass a written test after completing in-person classes (no on-line option);
- complete shooting range classes and pass a field test with at least a 95%;
- undergo a 'mental test' at a local hospital to screen for "readily detectable mental illness," including substance addiction. Successful applicants are given a medical certificate which they must present to the police;
- agree to a police investigation of the applicant and all relatives to ensure that none have criminal records or are members of "aggressive" political activist groups;

If even *one* of the above criteria is not met, a license will be denied. All gun owners must provide proof that their weapons are securely stored in a locker, keep ammunition stored in a separate, locked safe, and give police a map of their residence showing exactly where these lockers are. The average penalty for violating any of Japan's strict laws about possession and usage is one year of imprisonment. Meanwhile in America "responsible" gun owners whine about basic background checks.

Do these laws work? Judge for yourself: in 2011 Japan had a total of 11 firearm homicides and 15 firearm suicides.

And yes, they have sword control too.

*Norway*

Patriotic freedom-loving opponents of U.S. gun regulation were overjoyed when, in 2011, a Norwegian gunman killed 69 people and injured 110 others. "See?" they cried triumphantly. "Their strict gun laws didn't prevent this" So much for not politicizing tragedy.

Just how strict are Norway's gun control laws? The rate of licensed firearm ownership is 9.77 per 100 people. These are almost exclusively rifles and shotguns, with only 3.7% owning handguns. Yet the total number of guns is estimated at 31.3 per 100 people. There's a discrepancy there. What's going on? Two things: 1) licensed owners often have several guns, and 2) roughly half of Norway's 1.3 million guns are unregistered. As we see again and again, laws are only effective when enforced.

Still, to put things in perspective: Norway had a total of 77 mass shooting fatalities between 2009-2013, compared to 277 here in the Land of the Free.

The important takeaway here is that the citizens and government of Norway took this mass shooting seriously. It was a devastating wake-up call that led to a) tightening enforcement of their existing gun laws, and b) memorializing the massacre in a permanent, meaningful way. Swedish artist Jonas Dahlberg was commissioned to create a monument symbolizing the lives lost as "a <u>wound</u> within nature itself."

Imagine if we did this in the U.S.: there'd be so many slices missing that our national landscape would look like a comb.

CHAPTER 3

# *"Knives, hammers, baseball bats, etc. are used as murder weapons more often than guns!"*

Every one of these "alternative" murder weapons is designed for a primary purpose other than killing or injuring a living target, and have a lower rate lethality than guns.

As we've seen, guns are the deadliest choice of weapon. The chances of a "successful" suicide or homicide fatality are much higher with a gun than with any other method.

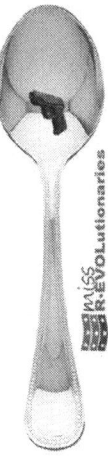

"I READ A JAW-DROPPING ONLINE DEFENSE OF THESE WEAPONS FROM A CALIFORNIA WOMAN RECENTLY. GUNS, SHE SAID, ARE JUST TOOLS. LIKE SPOONS, SHE SAID. WOULD YOU OUTLAW SPOONS SIMPLY BECAUSE SOME PEOPLE USE THEM TO EAT TOO MUCH? LADY, LET'S SEE YOU TRY TO KILL TWENTY SCHOOLKIDS WITH A FUCKING SPOON."

Stephen King

December 14, 2012: a gunman kills 20 first-graders and six adults at Sandy Hook Elementary School in Newtown, Connecticut, using an AR-15.

That same day, a man uses a knife to stab 23 children and one teacher at Chenpeng Village Elementary School in China. They all lived.

 – *"If they didn't use a gun, they'd just use something else!"*

The Bad Guys, it seems, have an endless arsenal of hammers, knives, baseball bats, tennis rackets, chainsaws, bricks, umbrellas, chairs, shovels, bowling balls, prosthetic limbs, wheels of cheese…the list goes on and on. Yet they keep going out of their way to use guns! So odd! Maybe it's because they're usually small, easy to hide, and deliver the most lethal results. Or maybe it's because, in <u>at least 20 states</u>, they're easier to get legally than a driver's license, a shelter pet or Sudafed.

Of course anything can be a deadly weapon, but not everything can be a deadly weapon with a high rate of accuracy from a distance of up to <u>3 miles</u>. I would frankly rather you tried to kill me with a spoon.

Anti-regulation arguments try to minimize the devastating toll of American gun violence by focusing instead on specific *types* of firearms used in murders, as classified by the <u>FBI Crime Statistics</u>:

| Weapons | 2010 | 2011 | 2012 | 2013 | 2014 |
|---|---|---|---|---|---|
| Total | 13,164 | 12,795 | 12,888 | 12,253 | 11,961 |
| Total firearms | 8,874 | 8,653 | 8,897 | 8,454 | 8,124 |
| Handguns | 6,115 | 6,251 | 6,404 | 5,782 | 5,562 |
| Rifles | 367 | 332 | 298 | 285 | 248 |
| Shotguns | 366 | 362 | 310 | 308 | 262 |
| Other guns | 93 | 97 | 116 | 123 | 93 |
| Firearms, type not stated | 1,933 | 1,611 | 1,769 | 1,956 | 1,959 |
| Knives or cutting instruments | 1,732 | 1,716 | 1,604 | 1,490 | 1,567 |
| Blunt objects (clubs, hammers, etc.) | 540 | 502 | 522 | 428 | 435 |
| Personal weapons (hands, fists, feet, etc.)[1] | 769 | 751 | 707 | 687 | 660 |

While the rest of us are processing the fact that guns were used in 2/3 of all homicides in 2014, anti-regulation nuts gleefully point out that that rifles killed a mere 248 people that year. Also knives were used more than shotguns, so therefore shotguns aren't a problem.

We DO have knife control; it's called, "Don't bring that fucking knife in here, you idiot." We restrict *all kinds* of objects, lethal and nonlethal. Try bringing a chainsaw into a library and see what happens. For that matter, try bringing a video camera to a concert, or a pen into a rare documents archive. Yet somehow it's a "right" to bring guns into stadiums, zoos, schools, restaurants, movie theaters, bars, bowling alleys, roller rinks, coffee shops, playgrounds and even churches.

If all these other objects are so much more dangerous than guns, why not get one of those for protection instead? You don't even need a permit to carry a concealed spoon.

CHAPTER 4

# *"Car accidents, falls, drownings, etc. kill more people each year than guns!"*

This is a favorite diversionary tactic of ammosexuals, and is meant to persuade you that the entire "problem" isn't really a problem at all.

> The 1938 stage play Gas Light tells the story of a husband who attempts to drive his wife insane by distorting her perceptions of reality – including turning down the gas lights in their home and then insisting the lights are not dimmed, even when she insists they are. This is where we get the term <u>gaslighting</u>, which is "a form of psychological abuse in which false information is presented to the victim with the intent of making him/her doubt his/her own memory and perception."

"Swimming pools are much more dangerous than guns when you carefully analyze the data," gun-humper sites proclaim smugly.

**CAUTION: gaslighting!**

"WHAT problem?"

This is a favorite diversionary tactic of ammosexuals: trying to claim there *is* no gun violence epidemic. It's all hysterical liberal-media anti-gun propaganda designed to usher in the New World Order or some crazy shit.

In 2014, When Target came under pressure to prohibit the open carry of firearms in its stores, the internet was aflame with gaslighting: "Are you scared of swimming pools too? You wouldn't boycott them over swimming pools, and those are way more dangerous!"

Once your head stops spinning from the sheer stupidity of this argument…it's ok, take a minute…you can point out that it's not valid to compare accidents and homicides. Remember, accidental/negligent gun deaths are no more than 1% of the total. The 3,868 <u>accidental drownings</u> each year far outnumber the 505 <u>accidental/negligent</u> shootings.

But simply arguing numbers misses the point; "outnumber" doesn't mean "outweigh." Just because more people accidentally drown than are accidentally/negligently shot doesn't mean we should just forget about trying to do anything to prevent drownings.

Imagine if, for some reason, Target decided to put a swimming pool in the middle of each of its stores. They'd also put a gate around it, have trained and certified lifeguards on duty, enforce safety rules, provide life preservers and keep emergency first-aid supplies on hand. They would be subject to regular inspections by third parties, and wouldn't cry that their freedoms were being trampled on. They wouldn't insist that you "just trust them."

No Good Guy has ever had their bathtub "accidentally" discharge in a public place. People who die in falls very seldom take bystanders down with them. We do everything we can to put safety measures in place to prevent deadly accidents, or at least minimize their damage. We pass – and enforce – laws regulating cars, swimming pools, furniture, toys, drugs, etc.

The idea that one deadly threat should be ignored in favor of an even deadlier threat is absurd. It's like saying that heart disease <u>kills more people</u> than cancer, so we shouldn't waste time or money fighting cancer until we've got that heart disease thing taken care of.

CHAPTER 5

# *Crime and punishment*

*"Strict gun laws = more violent crime, permissive gun laws = less violent crime."*

States with strong, consistently enforced gun laws have much lower rates of gun violence than states with permissive firearm laws.

Quick, which state has the most gun deaths? You might be tempted to guess Illinois, since gunlickers love to point to Chicago as an example of gun control's "failure." But it's not (more on that later).

Measuring gun deaths isn't always clear cut (and certain folks go out of their way to make it harder). There's the total *number* of firearm deaths, and then there's the *rate* of firearm deaths. Let's look at a couple of representative examples:

**California**: population 38.8 million, strict gun laws **Virginia**: population 8.36 million, loose gun laws

If we go by population alone, we might reasonably expect California to have a higher total of gun deaths than Virginia. If we give any weight to the "more laws=more crime arguments," we might even predict that California is *more* dangerous...especially since Virginia is the NRA's home state, so it's got to be crawling with Good Guys keeping everyone safe, right?

Alas, the evidence doesn't support either of these conclusions.

| California Mortality Data | Deaths | Rate** | U.S. Deaths | U.S. Rate*** |
|---|---|---|---|---|
| Firearm Deaths | 2935 | 7.4 | 33390 | 10.2 |

| Virginia Mortality Data | Deaths | Rate** | U.S. Deaths | U.S. Rate*** |
|---|---|---|---|---|
| Firearm Deaths | 885 | 10.3 | 33390 | 10.2 |

Yes, the total number of CA's firearm deaths is higher than VA's, because it's a bigger state. But when you compare the rate of gun deaths per 100 people, it becomes clear that your chances of getting shot are significantly higher in VA. Their rate of gun deaths is a bit *over* the nationwide average, while CA's is comfortably under it.

**American's shootiest states:**

| State | 2013 gun ownership |
|---|---|
| Arizona | 32.3% |
| Alaska | 61.7 |
| Wyoming | 53.8 |
| Louisiana | 44.5 |
| Montana | 52.3 |
| Arkansas | 57.9 |
| Virginia | 29.3 |
| Kentucky | 42.9 |
| Florida | 32.5 |
| Nevada | 37.5 |
| Maine | 22.6 |
| Mississippi | 42.8 |
| Idaho | 56.9 |
| New Mexico | 49.9 |
| Alabama | 48.9 |

# BUSTING GUN NUTS

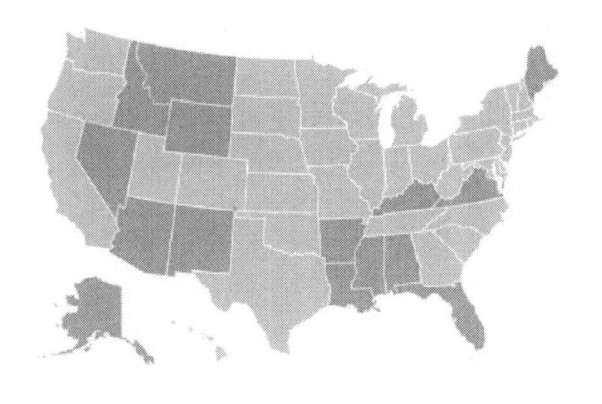

1. Arizona
2. Alaska
3. Wyoming
4. Louisiana
5. Montana
6. Arkansas
7. Virginia
8. Kentucky
9. Florida
10. Nevada
11. Maine
12. Mississippi
13. Idaho
14. New Mexico
15. Alabama

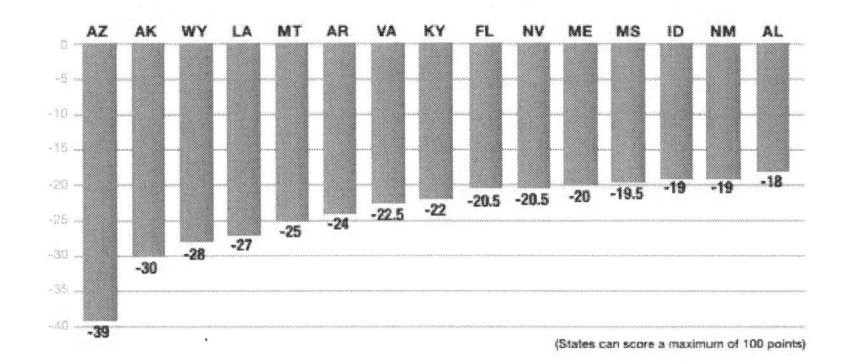

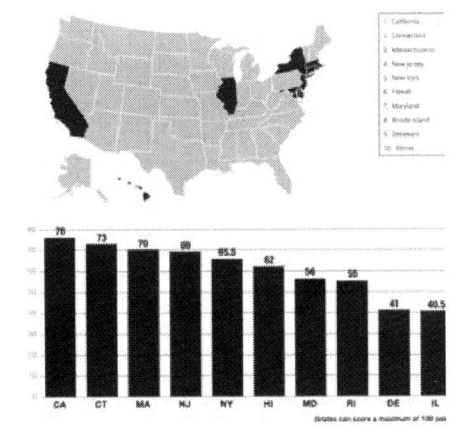

| State | AZ | AK | WY | LA | MT | AR | VA | KY | FL | NV | ME | MS | ID | NM | AL |
|---|---|---|---|---|---|---|---|---|---|---|---|---|---|---|---|
| Score | -39 | -30 | -28 | -27 | -25 | -24 | -22.5 | -22 | -20.5 | -20.5 | -20 | -19.5 | -19 | -19 | -18 |

(States can score a maximum of 100 points)

**America's safest states:**

| State | 2013 gun ownership |
|---|---|
| California | 20.1% |
| Connecticut | 16.6 |
| Massachusetts | 22.6 |
| New Jersey | 11.3 |
| New York | 10.3 |
| Hawaii | 45.1 |
| Maryland | 20.7 |
| Rhode Island | 5.8 |
| Delaware | 5.2 |
| Illinois | 26.2 |

| | CA | CT | MA | NJ | NY | HI | MD | RI | DE | IL |
|---|---|---|---|---|---|---|---|---|---|---|
| Score | 78 | 73 | 70 | 69 | 65.3 | 62 | 56 | 55 | 41 | 40.5 |

(States can score a maximum of 100 pts)

On the whole, it looks like the states with higher rates of gun ownership have <u>more gun deaths</u>, and lower gun ownership generally correlates with fewer gun deaths.

But wait...what's up with Hawaii? Nearly half its population owns guns, yet their rate of gun violence is very low. Maine's gun ownership rate is identical to Massachusetts, yet they're on two different lists. So what's going on?

The answer, not surprisingly, is: LAWS.

Brady's <u>expanded state scorecard</u> covers three category descriptions:

1) Keeping guns out of the hands of dangerous people (including universal background checks);

2) Stopping the supply of crime guns;

3) Contributing to our national gun violence problem.

Hawaii's gun laws are strong enough to rate a B-plus from the <u>Brady Campaign</u>, while California gets an A-minus. Maine and Virginia both get an F...as do 24 other states.

Again and again, no matter which sources you consult, you find the "usual suspects" of states with the most gun violence. The undeniable conclusion (by every measure except the gun lobby's) is that more guns = more gun violence.

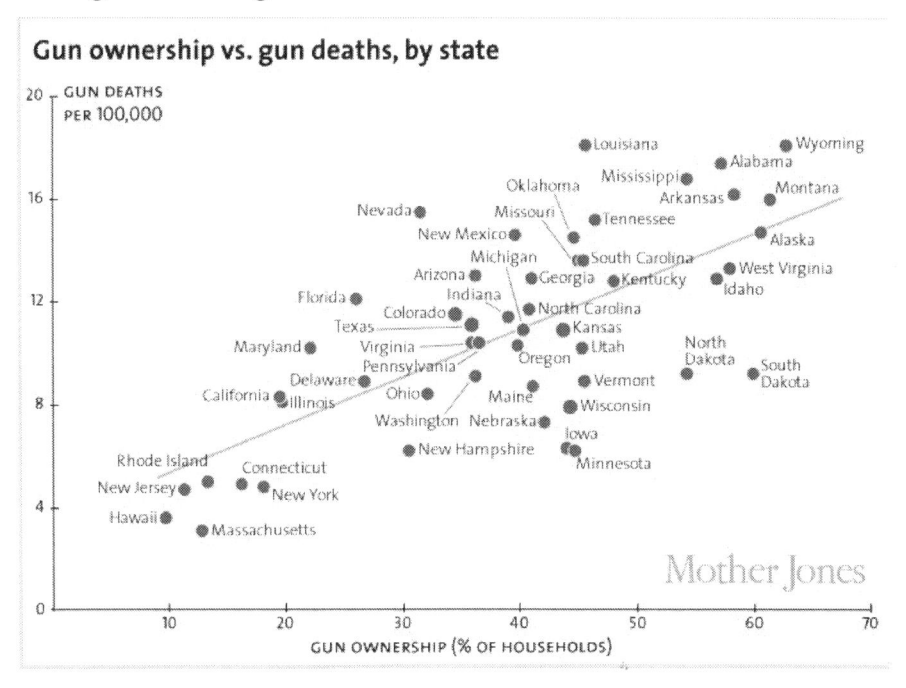

**Gun ownership vs. gun deaths, by state**

*[Scatter plot from Mother Jones showing gun deaths per 100,000 (y-axis, 0 to 20) against gun ownership as % of households (x-axis, 10 to 70) for each U.S. state. States with low gun ownership and low gun deaths include Hawaii, New Jersey, Massachusetts, Rhode Island, New York, and Connecticut. States with high gun ownership and high gun deaths include Wyoming, Alabama, Montana, Alaska, West Virginia, Louisiana, and Mississippi. A positive trend line shows correlation between gun ownership and gun deaths.]*

But state borders aren't bulletproof. The lack of any substantive federal firearms laws means that each state is pretty much on its own – or at the mercy of its neighbors.

CHAPTER 6

# "Chicago is the murder capital of the U.S.!" + "Chicago has some of the strictest gun laws in the country" = "Chicago proves gun control doesn't work!

Chicago's gun violence is nowhere near the worst in the nation, but illegal trafficking and poorly-enforced laws ensure that specific communities are at disproportionate risk.

Also, laws do not cause crime.

Chicago is <u>nowhere near</u>" the "murder capital" of the U.S.; in fact, it doesn't even make the list of top ten most dangerous U.S. major cities. The <u>2014 FBI crime statistics</u> bear this out:

**Violent crime per 100,000 people (murder, rape, robbery, assault)**

Detroit, Michigan 1988.63
Memphis, Tennessee 1740.51
Oakland, California 1685.39
St. Louis, Missouri 1678.73
Milwaukee, Wisconsin 1476.41
Baltimore, Maryland 1338.54
Cleveland, Ohio 1334.35
Stockton, California 1331.47
Indianapolis, Indiana 1254.66
Kansas City, Missouri 1251.45
**Chicago = 884.26**

**Murders per 100,000 people (all weapons)**

St. Louis, Missouri 49.91
Detroit, Michigan 43.52
New Orleans, Louisiana 38.75
Baltimore, Maryland 33.84
Newark, New Jersey 33.32
Buffalo, New York 23.22
Pittsburgh, Pennsylvania 22.43
Memphis, Tennessee 21.38
Atlanta, Georgia 20.47
Cincinnati, Ohio 20.16
**Chicago = 15**

And these are only the cities with populations over 250,000. When you adjust all murder rates by population, smaller cities like East St. Louis, IL or Flint, MI are far more dangerous.

This does NOT mean that Chicago – or any city- "wins" or "loses" the title of "Most Dangerous." The point is not to pin that award on any one city, but to provide pieces of a much larger puzzle.

What about shootings specifically? The answer is that there is no clear answer. Chicago does have the second-highest *number* of major city shootings per year, though this raw figure is not adjusted for population. Unlike other cities with high rates of gun violence (Jackson, MI, Boise, ID), Chicago takes its gun violence problem seriously, and dedicates resources to studying and accurately reporting all data.

CDC data on shootings from 2006-07 and 2009-10 reveal some highly disturbing trends:

- The vast majority of Chicago's shootings are concentrated in specific areas – particularly low-income neighborhoods with large populations of racial and ethnic minorities.

- Chicago's rate of shootings among adults remained at 6 per 100,000 people for both years, but the rate of fatal shootings of youths age 10-19 was an astonishing 9.3 and 7.9, respectively.

*"In short, it's probably impossible to know how much of an outlier Chicago might be. There are certainly more incidents of gun violence than in many or most cities, but we don't know how many. Detroit appears to have had a worse year in 2014, but lacks the political significance – and attention - of Obama's Chicago."*

Guns are the number-one choice of murder weapon in Chicago by far, just like everywhere else. 90% of Chicago's murder victims are male, and 75% are Black. In other words, you are much, MUCH more likely to be shot and/or killed if you are a black male under age 19 living on the west or south sides.

> "But it's just gang violence!" –
>
> This is what people say to reassure themselves that they're safe, that it won't happen to them, that the thousands of people shot and killed in Chicago (or anywhere else) each year must have brought it on themselves somehow.
>
> It allows them to feel morally superior about turning their backs on the destruction of families, communities, children and bystanders caught in the crossfire. At best, it is thinly veiled racism packaged as victim-blaming; at worst it perpetuates the cycle of violence that disproportionately affects Black and Latino lives.
>
> Don't all lives matter?

Notice the paradox at work here: gunhumpers will claim Chicago has the worst gun problem in America, but at the same time It's not really a problem because it's mostly "black on black" crime. They ignore the river of illegally-trafficked guns that create the problem in the first place.

How strict are Chicago's much-touted gun laws? They used to deserve their reputation as among the toughest in the nation, but "courts have overturned or gutted many of them in recent years." Plus there's not much any city can do about its close neighbors.

*Where do Chicago's crime guns come from?*

**Out of state (60%):** Illinois borders three states with notoriously weak gun laws: Wisconsin, Indiana and Missouri. These account for more than half of all guns recovered in crimes...10% from gun-lovin' Indiana alone. Since Indiana basically has no gun laws whatsoever, many Chicagoans make a regular habit of driving 20 minutes across the state border to buy cheaper gas or cigarettes, illegal fireworks, and of course guns. Hoosiers can turn a tidy profit selling to Chicago's street gangs, without the inconvenience of a long commute.

Federal firearms trafficking laws and universal background checks would go a very long way toward reducing the carnage Chicago suffers at the hands of its neighbors (with a little help from Mississippi, Kentucky, Tennessee, Georgia, Ohio, Texas, Florida, Michigan, Iowa, Alabama and Arkansas).

**Right here at home (20%):** Almost 90% of all crime guns nationwide are traced back to a mere 5% of "bad apple" gun dealers. Chicago is an unfortunate embodiment of that problem. The three Illinois shops that sold at least one-fifth of guns used in crimes from 2009-2013 are:

- **Chuck's Gun Shop and Pistol Range** in Riverdale, IL sold 1,516 crime guns – almost *one per day* for the entire period of the study;
- **Midwest Guns** in Lyons, IL sold 659 – still too many to be "accidental;"
- **Shore Galleries** in Lincolnwood, IL sold 483.

Illinois gun dealers are not required to be licensed by the state, so there is zero accountability for selling a gun to someone who shouldn't have one. Mandatory state licensing for gun businesses (just as we have for restaurants, nail salons, dog groomers, yoga studios, etc.) would help prevent criminally negligent sales.

## How guns get to where they shouldn't be:

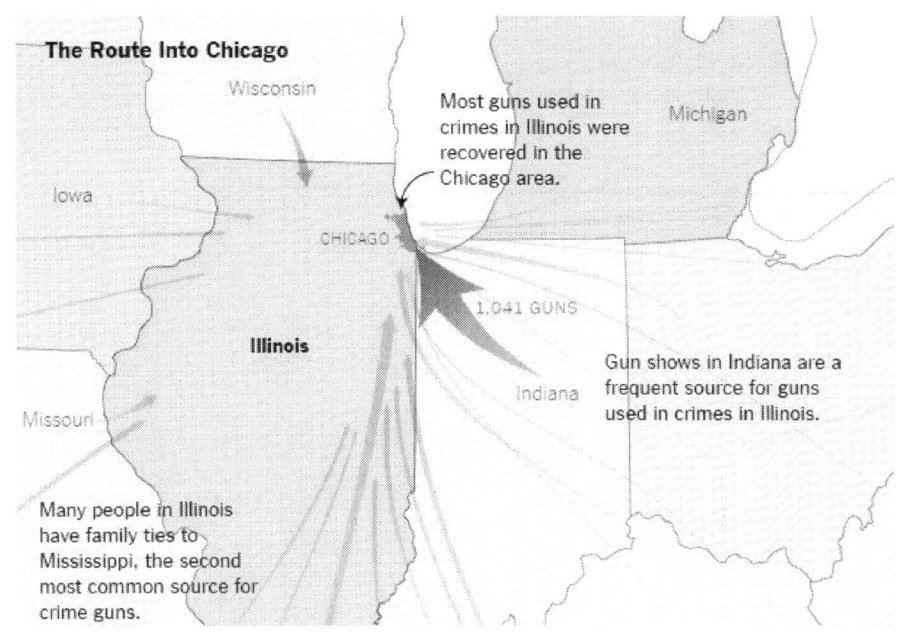

**The Route Into Chicago**

Wisconsin

Most guns used in crimes in Illinois were recovered in the Chicago area.

Michigan

Iowa

CHICAGO

1,041 GUNS

Illinois

Indiana

Gun shows in Indiana are a frequent source for guns used in crimes in Illinois.

Missouri

Many people in Illinois have family ties to Mississippi, the second most common source for crime guns.

CHAPTER 7

# *"Criminals don't follow laws!"*

No, criminals don't follow laws; that's what makes them criminals. This is a version of the nirvana fallacy - the idea that if something doesn't work 100% perfectly all the time, then it's no good and should be discarded. (Example: "We can't cure all types of cancer with 100% success, so we should give up on searching for a cure and just drink voodoo bullshit smoothies.")

**Gun control doesn't work because gun violence still happens!**

Yeah! Let's get rid of against murder, since people break those too.

Just as sexual assault needs to be understood more broadly than a masked Bad Guy jumping out of the bushes, it's equally ridiculous to think of "gun crime" solely in terms of masked Bad Guys robbing banks. Most people who commit gun homicides have some kind of criminal record. Domestic abuse, road rage, family disputes, relationship breakups, drunken arguments and cases of mistaken identity often turn deadly when someone has a gun in their hand – especially someone who should never have had one in the first place.

## A few reasons people shot other people in Oct., 2014

I like to play with my loaded gun while I watch The Walking Dead. I got fidgety while I was engrossed in the show and unintentionally shot my little brother to death. (TX, 10/19)

My friend jokingly slapped me in the face, so I jokingly shot her in the head with a gun I thought was unloaded. It wasn't. (FL, 10/4)

I was playing "gun tag" with a three-year-old child. He was pointing his toy gun at me, so I pointed my real, loaded handgun at him. I didn't really intend to shoot him, but I was drunk and I got carried away with the game. (MT, 10/22)

After Dad died, I wanted his tractor. My brother wanted it too, so I shot him in the head. (FL, 10/28)

My boyfriend brought a shotgun home and told me I needed to learn how to use it. So I shot him. (TX, 10/31)

I ordered some food at a restaurant. When the cashier told me the price, I got upset. So I shot her repeatedly. (FL, 10/30)

I was asleep and my cousin started jumping on my bed to wake me up, so I shot him to death. (PA, 10/14)

At a gathering after a funeral, I asked a woman for her phone number. She said no, so I shot her and five of her family members. (MI, 10/4)

I was racing radio-controlled cars with another man. We got into an argument about who won the race, so I shot at him. (TN, 10/16)

I signed a contract to restore this guy's old truck, but when I told him it was going to cost more than I had estimated, he said he wouldn't pay. So I shot him. (KY, 10/24)

When I found my house had been burglarized, I had a tantrum on my front lawn. Neighbors came out to watch me. A thirteen-year-old started laughing, so I drew my gun and shot him nine times. (IN, 10/24)

PARENTS AGAINST GUN VIOLENCE

When you extend the criminals-don't-follow-laws argument to its logical conclusion, you see why it doesn't work for...well, anything, really. We can't stop all drunk driving, so let's repeal the laws and speed limits and let people do whatever they want. Let's take the locks off our doors and get rid of seat belts and safety rails and smoke detectors, pull out all the traffic signals and no-smoking signs. No more airport security screening either, because people will ignore those laws too. There's nothing we can do about pedophilia, so let's not have sex offender registries or AMBER alerts. Let's stop studying traffic-related deaths, because we all know the next step is a total ban on cars, and not bother with addiction programs anymore, because we'll end up with Prohibition.

But anti-regulation extremists like this argument because it's so easy to tailor to *any* proposed solution: "Background checks won't stop all dangerous people from getting guns," "Banning assault weapons won't stop all mass shootings," and so on. When they pause to spit their chew, you can say: "You're absolutely right - it won't stop *all* of them. Would you settle for 'most?'"

CHAPTER 8

# "We don't need new gun laws – we just need to enforce the laws already on the books!"

Sure, okay! Let's start by locking up every sheriff who refuses to do his or her (but mostly his) job in the name of "defending gun rights." While we're at it, we can recall or impeach every elected official who receives money from the gun lobby in exchange for blocking legislation to enforce existing gun laws. Let's give the Bureau of Alcohol, Tobacco, Firearms and Explosives the funding and support it needs to do its fucking job.

> "One of the most frustrating things that I hear is when people say -- who are opposed to any further laws -- 'Why don't you just enforce the laws that are on the books?' And those very same members of Congress then cut [Bureau of Alcohol, Tobacco, Firearms and Explosives] budgets to make it impossible to enforce the law."
>
> – Barack Obama, "Guns in America," Jan. 7, 2016

Everyone understands that laws are not supernatural force fields that magically repel crime. It's not like holding up a cross to a vampire. Laws are effective only when they

a) exist

b) are consistently enforced, and

c) carry real consequences.

Most gun laws "are written in a way that makes them impossible to enforce -- intentionally," says Sarah Trumble, senior policy counsel of Americans for Gun Safety, which conducted the study. "They're too vague to prosecute, the standards are too high to meet, [and] the penalties are too low to be a deterrent."

In other words, prosecutors don't prosecute because prosecutors like to win, not lose. The rate of federal gun crime prosecutions is at almost a record low - and it wasn't that great to begin with. The AGS study found that, between 2000-2002, a grand total of 2% of federal gun crimes were prosecuted. You can't blame that on Obama. It was George W. Bush who focused on two particular statutes to increase gun prosecutions: possession of a firearm by a felon and possession of a firearm while committing another federal crime.

These two laws alone make up 85% of prosecution cases, suggesting that no one anywhere is trying very hard to enforce the other 20 or so federal gun laws.

And when lawmakers – even presidents - do make efforts to enforce gun laws, they face an onslaught of opposition and threats.

Let's look at an example:

*Laws requiring criminal background checks for all gun sales, public and private (no loopholes):* Nearly half the U. S. thinks we already have universal background checks – including some gun reform supporters who live in states with strong gun laws and wrongly assume the rest of the country has them too (looking at you, Massachusetts).

The 1993 Brady Background Check law is not – and CANNOT be -- universally enforced. This is because of a single very big loophole – one that allows 40% of all gun purchases to go undetected. This is the "gun show loophole," which lets "private sales and transfers" by unlicensed dealers off the hook. It was a concession to the gun lobby, a token of good faith which they repaid by urging their membership to subvert the tyranny of jack-booted government thugs by making unregulated purchases at gun shows (and now on the internet).

> If you possibly can, read the entire study on "The Enforcement Gap." If you don't have time to read the whole thing, read the Executive Summary. If you don't have time to read the Executive Summary, at least read the Table of Contents:
>
> **Finding I**: Overall prosecutions for violations of federal gun laws do not in any way reflect the number of federal gun crimes committed.
>
> **Finding II**: Despite a massive black market in crime guns, the five major federal laws to combat gun trafficking are virtually ignored.
>
> **Finding III**: Corrupt gun dealers are rarely prosecuted.
>
> **Finding IV**: Federal laws designed to keep guns out of the hands of kids and away from schools are almost never enforced.
>
> **Finding V**: There is one federal prosecution for every 1,000 stolen firearms.
>
> **Finding VI**: Individuals who lie on the criminal background check form are rarely punished.
>
> **Finding VII**: Although police routinely recover crime guns with obliterated serial numbers, prosecutions are rare.
>
> **Finding VIII**: Nearly all federal prosecutions involve those with previous criminal histories in possession of a firearm or for the use of a firearm in a federal crime of violence or drugs.

It is common to hear claims that the gun show loophole does not exist. The short answer, of course, is "<u>Bullshit</u>."

The long answer to this is UCLA Constitutional Law professor Adam Winkler's <u>explanation</u> of this term as a misnomer: "It should be the 'private sale loophole' or the 'background check loophole.' ... The reason people talk about gun shows is that they are easily accessible marketplaces for people who don't want to be subject to a background check to find non-licensed gun sellers."

So go ahead and say that instead, if it helps.

CHAPTER 9

# *The SECOND AMENDMENT!!!!*

Guess what the NRA has on the wall in the lobby of its fortress in Virginia?

If you guessed the Second Amendment, you're right...sort of.

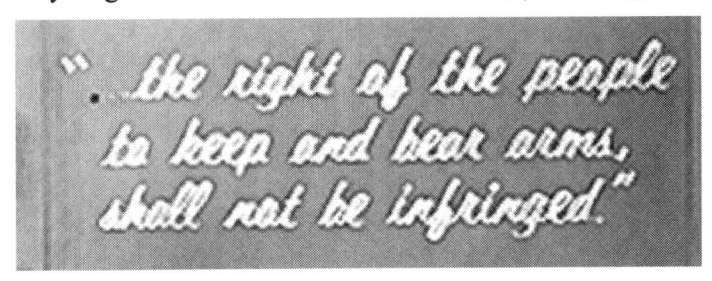

> "...the right of the people to keep and bear arms, shall not be infringed."

*Notice anything missing?*

WELL-REGULATED, THEY FORGOT THE PART ABOUT WELL-REGULATED. The full text of the Second Amendment to the Constitution, in its entirety, is as follows:

*"A well regulated Militia, being necessary to the security of a free State, the right of the people to keep and bear Arms, shall not be infringed."*

Jonny   SHALL NOT BE INFRINGED
Like · Reply · 6 hrs

　　Richard　　So felons should have guns?
　　Like · Reply · 👍 5 · 6 hrs

　　**Betsy F. Yerguns**　I'll see your "shall not be infringed" and raise you a "well-regulated." Also your caps key is stuck.
　　Like · Reply · 👍 5 · 5 hrs · Edited

*Uh oh...looks like the Constitution actually* supports *gun control!*

Let's take a closer look at these 27 words, starting with the ones the NRA prefers to ignore.

**"Well-regulated"**: Implies regulation by government—state, federal, or both. There's plenty of room for debate about intent, limits, and responsibilities, but there's the word "regulation" right there, inked onto yellowed parchment.

There were colonial gun laws regulating loaded firearms in buildings, gunpowder, firing guns in public spaces, and prohibiting firearms ownership by slaves, Catholics and "dissenters." These were to prevent and (dare I say) control "great Damages ... frequently done on [holidays] by persons going House to House, with Guns and other Firearms and being often intoxicated with Liquor." A 1792 federal law required every eligible man to keep a military-style gun and ammunition for his service in the citizen militia, and report for frequent musters—"where their guns would be inspected and, yes, registered on public rolls."

**"Militia"**: Article I, section 8, clause 15 of the Constitution ("the Militia Clause") grants to Congress the power "to provide for calling forth the militia to execute the laws of the union, suppress insurrections and repel Invasions" and "to provide for organizing, arming, and disciplining, the militia."

In Federalist No. 29, Alexander Hamilton laid out pretty clearly what a "well-regulated militia" is and does: all militia members must undergo rigorous training to attain "proficiency in military functions" and perform the "operations of an army," serve as ordered under the ultimate command of the president, and be subject to military discipline. If this sounds like the National Guard, that's because the 18th century militia performed a similar function.

BUSTING GUN NUTS

*A well-regulated militia.*

So now that it's 2016, and the U.S. government has a standing army and a National Guard, tanks, helicopters, fighter jets, drones, sea-to-land missiles, bunker-busters and other top-secret weapons *that we don't even know about*, tell me again how a bunch of untrained, unvetted neckbeards with felony records are going to protect us all from government tyranny by toting their AR-15s into Starbucks.

*Not a militia.*

Remember 2008? Those were the days: Sarah Palin had just come along, the Pope was an ex-Hitler Youth, China sent us a bunch of melamine, and you could sort of forget about the global economic meltdown while watching *Breaking Bad*.

THAT'S how long it's been since the SCOTUS ruled that the Second Amendment guarantees the individual right to own firearms.

CHAPTER 10

# *The Founding Fathers: fact and fiction*

The Federalists and Anti-Federalists went head-to-head over whether an armed populace would be able to resist federal oppression. In the end, the final draft of the Second Amendment "conceded nothing to the Anti-Federalists' desire to sharply curtail the power of the federal government."

In other words, Big Government won. And Big Government, in this case, meant big names: Jefferson. Madison. Hamilton. Washington.

Today the small-government militia types who call themselves "sovereign citizens" (which sounds so much better than "terrorists" or "traitors") like to trot out popular but entirely imaginary quotes that supposedly prove the Founding Fathers were gun-sucking man-babies just like them:

**FUN FACT!** Shay's Rebellion, that boring little grey sidebar of text in your history book, was an armed uprising of Massachusetts farmers that scared the Founding Fathers shitless. Washington called it "a cloud of evils which threatened...the tranquility of the Union." Afterward, the Constitutional Convention of 1787 was called—not to say, "Hey, good job with your attempted armed overthrow of us," but to *strengthen* the power of the central government to deter further such naughtiness.

"Ferfucksake, we were talking about musket balls, not 13.3 goddamn bullets per second."

- President George Washington

— 57 —

*"A free people ought not only be armed and disciplined, but they should have sufficient arms and ammunition to maintain a status of independence from any who might attempt to abuse them, which would include their own government."* Alas, the boy who could not tell a lie would not be at all pleased with posterity attributing this lie to him. What Washington actually said in his First Annual Address to Congress was, "A free people ought not only to be armed, **but disciplined; to which end a uniform and well-digested plan is requisite."** Eh, close enough.

*"Those who hammer their guns into plowshares will plow for those who do not."*—Also fake, but is usually attributed either to Thomas Jefferson or James Madison…both of whom made a point of banning firearms on the University of Virginia campus.

*"When governments fear the people, there is liberty. When people fear the government, there is tyranny."* Jefferson never actually said this or anything like it, but to this day gunhumpers insist the Founding Fathers' promise to America was, "Hey, if you don't like the job we're doing, you can shoot us, k?"

Jefferson is a favorite subject of 100% bullshit quotes, including:

- *"Dissent is the highest form of patriotism."* (In a way this one makes a good point, but not in the shooting kind of way.)
- *"The beauty of the Second Amendment is that it will not be needed until they try to take it."* (Whaddaya mean "they?" Aren't you them?)
- *"Free men do not ask permission to bear arms."* (The "permission slip" metaphor was also a favorite of George W. Bush.)
- *"If a law is unjust, a man is not only right to disobey it, he is obligated to do so."* (See comment under first bullet point)
- *"No freeman shall ever be debarred the use of arms."*
- *"The strongest reason for the people to retain the right to keep and bear arms is, as a last resort, to protect themselves against tyranny in government."*

BUSTING GUN NUTS

> ***FUN FACT!*** *At the time the Constitution was framed, firearms consisted of <u>muzzle-loading muskets and flintlock rifles</u>. To load a musket, all you had to do was hold your ten-pound gun upright in one hand, and with the other hand take out your powder-horn and measure the right amount of powder to pour down the barrel, then use your finger to push a lead ball into the barrel and ram it down against the powder with a ramrod. Then it was just a simple matter of pouring a finer grade of powder from a different powder horn into the flash pan before you pulled back the hammer, closing the frizzen to keep powder from spilling out of the pan, aiming and firing. A well-trained solider could fire 2 to 3 shots a minute. The higher the caliber, the more labor-intensive the loading process was. Eventually, though, powder residue builds up in the barrel and makes it harder to use.*
>
> *Easy, right? You could totally kill <u>26 people in five minutes</u> with one of those.*

You can amaze your friends and confound your enemies by dropping a truth bomb next time you encounter someone spouting this fucking nonsense.

**A MILLION TIMES MORE EFFECTIVE THAN VOTING**

## BETSY F. YERGUNS

*I cannot imagine why people are getting their panties in a twist over implicit threats to shoot the president, unless it has something to do with U.S. Code Title 18 871*

**Gun Rights**
19 hours ago

Why is that when I post stuff about the American revolutionaries using guns to get freedom it's all positive feedback, but when I post something about John Wilkes Booth using a gun to defend freedom everyone freaks out?

CHAPTER 11

# *Two centuries of interpretation*

The Second Amendment, like every single other amendment, is subject to interpretation. It is not, as one Indiana lawmaker put it, "an immaculate conception." Indeed, it's fucked in all kinds of ways.

"Much has changed since 1791," Nelson Lund and Adam Winkler point out. "State-based militia organizations were eventually incorporated into the federal military structure...[Today] virtually no one thinks that an armed populace could defeat those forces in battle."

Well, virtually no one except these assholes:

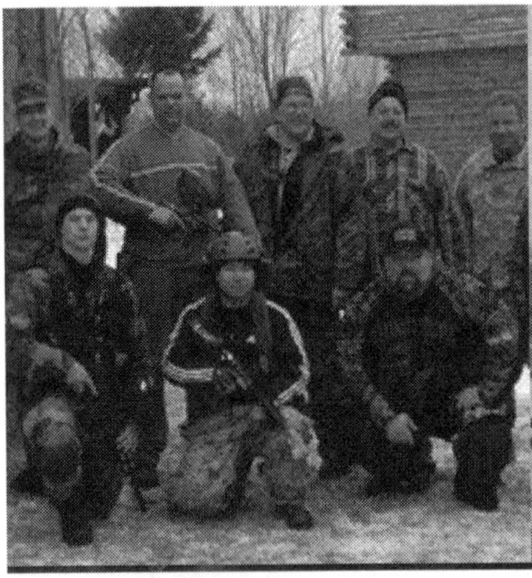

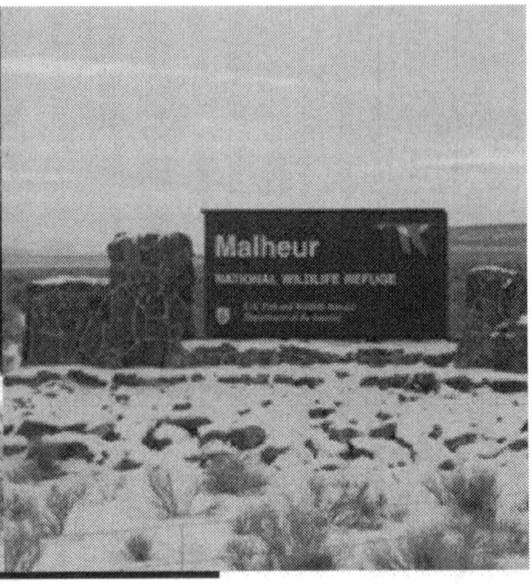
Malheur
NATIONAL WILDLIFE REFUGE

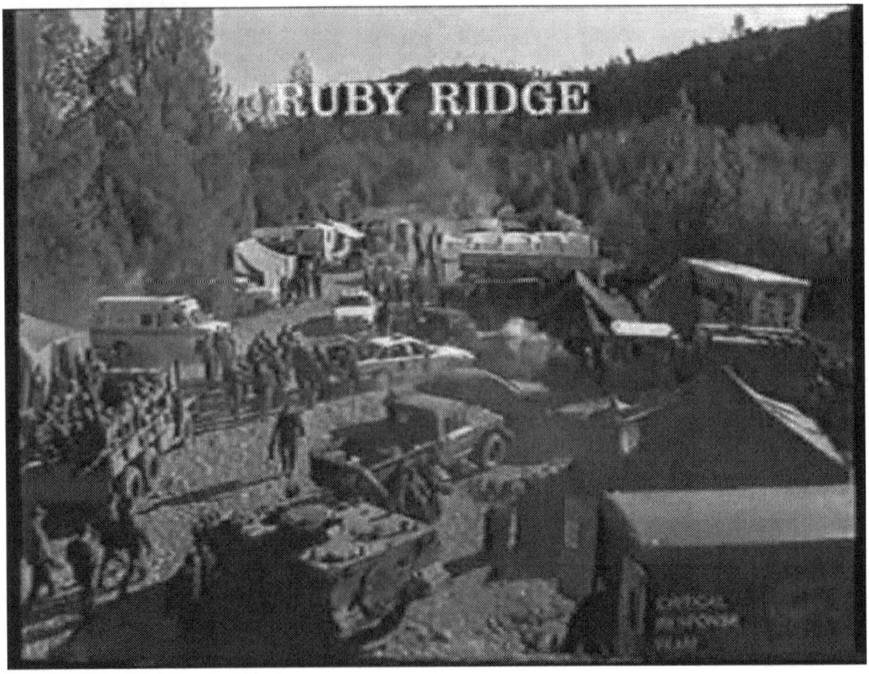
RUBY RIDGE

A stroll through any gun-flavored Facebook group or online comment thread will be full of plenty of examples of this revisionist, violence-inciting, racist, misogynistic, anti-Semitic faux-patriotism. There has also, since 2008, been a mysterious uptick in the number of ~~crybaby cowards~~ "sovereign citizens," "whose adherents hold truly bizarre, complex antigovernment beliefs...[including] that they get to decide which laws to obey and which to ignore."

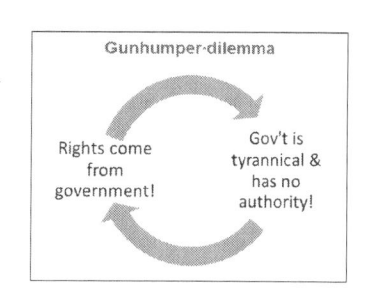

The insurrectionist theory (which is not popular among legal scholars) is a deliberate twisting of the framers' idea that "preserving the right to bear arms might help the populace form a militia that could fight a standing government army that *turned against the people.*" Judge Alex Kozinski called the concept a "doomsday provision, one designed for those exceptionally rare circumstances where all other rights have failed." Darrell Miller, Professor of Constitutional Law at Duke University, stresses that taking up arms against the government "is borne of grave necessity and pressing oppression."

In other words, insurrection isn't something you whip out because your preferred candidate lost the election, or your cattle were confiscated after you illegally grazed them on public land, or you don't like paying taxes, or you think the Civil War is still on. When elected officials seize power and refuse to leave office, when the courts cannot count on enforcement of their laws, when the U.S. army is commanded to attack its own civilians, *then* we can begin to talk about the nuclear option of insurrection.

> "The problem with the insurrectionist theory is there is always someone who thinks that tyranny is in the present. "

Darrell Miller sums up the pasty-white privilege driving much of the anti-regulation movement: "When people think of the right to revolt, they think of Patrick Henry or Thomas Jefferson. They don't think about Malcolm X or the Black Panthers, even though the Black Panthers were quite open about the fact that they were arming themselves as a check on the police force."

**A quick rundown of Supreme Court rulings on gun rights and restrictions:**

*U.S. v. Cruikshank* (1875): "The right to bear arms is not granted by the Constitution; neither is it in any manner dependent upon that instrument for its existence."

*Presser v. Illinois* (1886): The Second Amendment is not incorporated through the Fourteenth Amendment, and is not enforceable against the states (this case, btw, upheld the Illinois' authority to prohibit ARMED PUBLIC PARADES).

*Miller v. Texas* (1894): The 2A does not prohibit state laws regulating the carry of firearms. U.S. v Miller (1939): upheld prohibitions on interstate trafficking of weapons, including specific types of firearms.

*D.C. v. Heller* (2008), Although it effectively struck down Washington, D.C.'s handgun ban. *Heller* established **only** that the federal government cannot prohibit citizens from having legally-owned firearms in their homes, though it did not take up the question of concealed carry – or any specific regulations whatsoever. The ruling clearly allows for - and even suggests - examples of "presumptively lawful" regulations that states might adopt. Because D.C. is under federal jurisdiction, it remained unclear whether this interpretation would also apply to the states.

*McDonald v Chicago* (2010) affirmed Heller's applicability and forced all states to allow concealed weapons, even if local ordinances prohibited it. (So much for small government and states' rights.) *McDonald* also reversed the precedent set by Presser, establishing that the 2A IS enforceable against the states, because the Equal Protection Clause of the 14A protected former slaves' right to keep and bear arms.

You can see the trend here: from the 19th through the early 21st century, gun laws have actually become less restrictive, moving *away* from federal control and toward a dangerous ideology that encourages and promotes armed violence as a first solution, not a last resort.

CHAPTER 12

# *The NRA - Before*

Once upon a time there was a noble civil rights organization of freedom-loving patriots who wanted to help the former slaves fight back against the Ku Klux Klan. They founded themselves on the Second Amendment and worked tirelessly to protect our God-given gun rights against even the slightest hint of infringement by "criminal-coddling do-gooders, borderline psychotics, as well as Communists and leftists who want to lead us into the one-world welfare state."

No, wait…let's try that again:

Once upon a time there was a group of former Union Army officers who were unhappy about what lousy shots their troops were. "The National Guard is to-day too slow in getting about [training] reform," they grumbled in an 1871 article in *Army and Navy Journal*. "An association should be organized in this city [New York] to promote and encourage rifle-shooting on a scientific basis." Britain, they pointed out, had already incorporated its many local shooting-club chapters into a national group that held marksmanship tournaments each year. "Let us have our rifle practice association," they said, "also a Wimbledon on American principles."

And so they did.

**So what went wrong?**

During its first hundred years the NRA was a nonpolitical sport club, whose stated purpose was "Firearms safety education, marksmanship training, [and] shooting for recreation." Congress formally recognized it in 1903, and appropriated funding for a bigger, broader tournament under direction of the War Department. NRA president Karl Frederick even testified before Congress in support of the National Firearms Act of 1934. When asked whether the proposed law violated any part of the Constitution, Frederick responded, "I have not given it any study from that point of view."

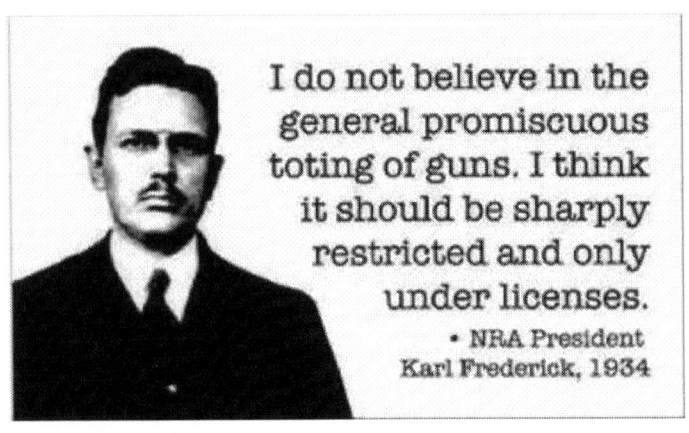

> I do not believe in the general promiscuous toting of guns. I think it should be sharply restricted and only under licenses.
> • NRA President Karl Frederick, 1934

In 1957, civil rights leader Robert Williams founded the Black Armed Guard under a charter granted by the NRA. The Ku Klux Klan had terrorized the NAACP chapter in Monroe, North Carolina to the point where only two members remained. Williams was careful, however, to obscure his race on the application. "I'm sure when we joined and the years after then, had they known we were a black group, they would have revoked our charter," his widow Mabel said.

"In the historic system of the South," Michael Waldman writes, "having a gun was a white prerogative." In fact, the idea of Negroes with guns alarmed the NRA so much that a rift began to form between the sane, moderate old guard and the paranoid, militant new. This rift widened after President John. F. Kennedy was shot by a maniac who purchased his bolt-action rifle through the mail. Even so, the official NRA leadership supported tighter gun laws: "The measure as a whole appears to be one that the sportsmen of America can live with," said executive vice-president Franklin L. Orth of one such bill. "We do not think that any sane American, who calls himself an American, can object to placing into this bill the instrument which killed the president of the United States,"

The key word here, of course, was "sane," which a growing faction of the NRA membership was proving not to be. The 1965 Dodd Bill (to limit mail-order sales on military surplus weapons) eventually passed despite strong opposition from the southern states.

> **Fun Fact!**
>
> The Senate Judiciary Committee rejected the Dodd bill on April 4, 1968...the very same afternoon Martin Luther King, Jr. was shot and killed.
>
> Later, when they approved a proposal to prohibit the sale of handguns by interstate mail, neither side was happy. "At best, it was a halfway measure, but its defenders held that it was better than nothing," historian <u>Richard Harris</u> said. ***"Others felt that its passage would give the public false comfort and thereby postpone for another generation necessary action."***

*"Negative response by the membership precipitated a subsequent reversal of direction by the NRA leadership"* is criminologist <u>William Vizzard</u>'s fancy way of saying that, once the rednecks got pissed off, shit began to go off the rails. "By 1965, the leadership and membership of the NRA divided along a fault line separating those tolerant of moderate increases in gun control from those opposed to any significant change in the law."

> "Although most of the committee's members did not want to incur the gun lobby's wrath by approving the bill, neither did they want to be charged with cowardice by their constituents, a majority of whom favored the bills."

The rise of the Black Panther Party and its <u>occupation of the California statehouse</u> in May 1967 further stoked the fear and paranoia among the good old law-abidin' southern boy anti-regulation gun owners.

> "Any hope of compromise between advocates of stricter gun control and the NRA ended after 1965." (Vizzard)

They huddled together in bunkers filled with canned food and back issues of *Guns & Ammo* that warned of the coming race war and government takeover. There was a series of shakeups at the highest levels of NRA leadership, culminating in what gunhumpers still reverently call the "Revolt at Cincinnati."

> "On May 21, 1977, and into the morning of May 22, a rump caucus of gun rights radicals took over the annual meeting of the National Rifle Association. The rebels wore orange-blaze hunting caps [and] spoke on walkie-talkies as they worked the floor of the sweltering convention hall.... The rebels saw the NRA leaders as elites who lacked the heart and conviction to fight against gun-control legislation.... The Old Guard NRA officers sat up front, on a dais, observing their demise."
>
> --*Washington Post*, "How the NRA's true believers converted a marksmanship group into a mighty gun lobby."

In a torturous parliamentary procedure that lasted until 4:00 a.m., the organization's bylaws were altered, the old Board of Directors voted out, and Harlan Carter installed as the new president of the NRA.

Carter, a longtime NRA board member and founding director of the new NRA lobbying unit (ILA), based his strategy on "a simple concept: *No compromise. No gun legislation.*"

CHAPTER 13

# *The NRA today*

The 1972 Republican party platform had pledged to "intensify efforts to prevent criminal access to all weapons, including special emphasis on cheap, readily-obtainable hand-guns . . . with such federal law as necessary."

The 1980 Republican party platform was basically a big "Fuck you" to any attempt at bringing some sanity back to America's gun laws. Ronald Reagan was the first presidential candidate to be endorsed by the newly-radicalized NRA. Or rather, by its lobbying arm, the NRA-ILA (Institute for Legislative Action

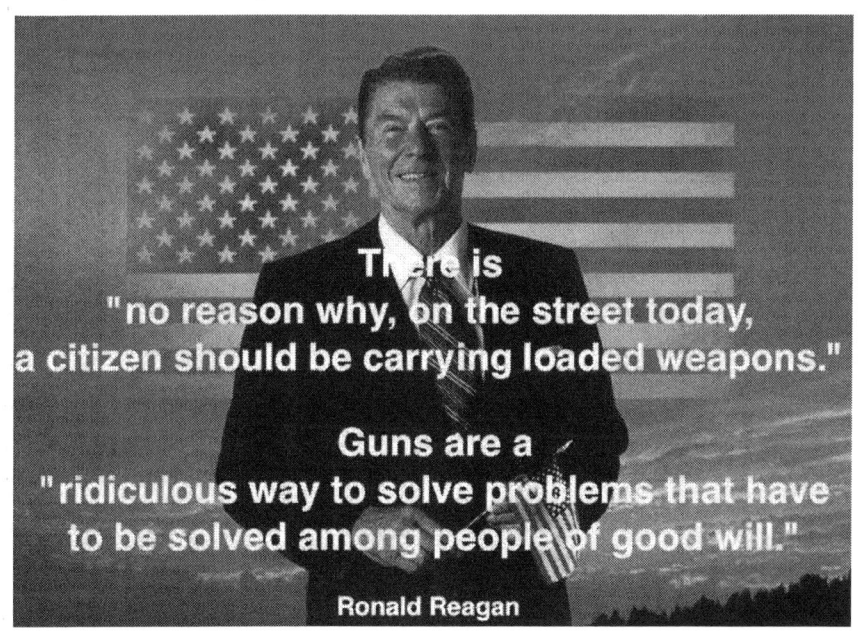

> There is "no reason why, on the street today, a citizen should be carrying loaded weapons."
>
> Guns are a "ridiculous way to solve problems that have to be solved among people of good will."
>
> **Ronald Reagan**

*This guy was actually fine with gun control.*

Altogether, the many-headed hydra that is the modern NRA pours <u>tens of millions of dollars</u> into buying off politicians, lobbying and other mysterious "outside spending" in order to defend your God-given right to shoot <u>unarmed black teenagers.</u> The group that was founded to promote firearms training and safety now backs <u>recall elections</u> targeting legislators who dare to support sensible gun law reform, <u>fights background checks</u> and <u>waiting periods</u> tooth and nail, sends its top lobbyists to kill <u>safe storage laws,</u> attempts to block confirmation of the president's <u>Surgeon General appointee,</u> leans over legislators' shoulders to <u>weaken gun laws</u> and push racist <u>"Stand Your Ground"</u> laws in more than half the states, <u>cranks out lies</u> to terrify the gullible into buying more and more and more guns...... and makes <u>over $300 million a year</u> from it, <u>tax-free.</u>

> How much did the gun lobby pay YOUR representatives to oppose gun reform?
>
> Find a complete list of NRA "donations" <u>here!!</u>

## THINGS THE NRA SAYS WE CAN'T HAVE:

- **Federal research on gun violence**: The <u>Dickey Amendment,</u> passed in 1996, ensures that "none of the funds made available for injury prevention and control at the Centers for Disease Control and Prevention (CDC) may be used to advocate or promote gun control." This is why there's no comprehensive central database of information on shooters and shootings; the best we can do is patch it together from statistical reports and privately-funded studies. (For an extra dose of irony, the same NRA lackey who sponsored the bill now has <u>deep regrets</u>.)
- **Universal background checks**: The NRA <u>fought the Brady bill</u> for six years before it passed. These days it falsely <u>takes credit</u> for the limited background check laws, while denying

the existence of the "private sale" loophole that allows 40% of all gun purchases to go unchecked.

- **Bans** on high-capacity magazines and armor-piercing ("cop killer") bullets.

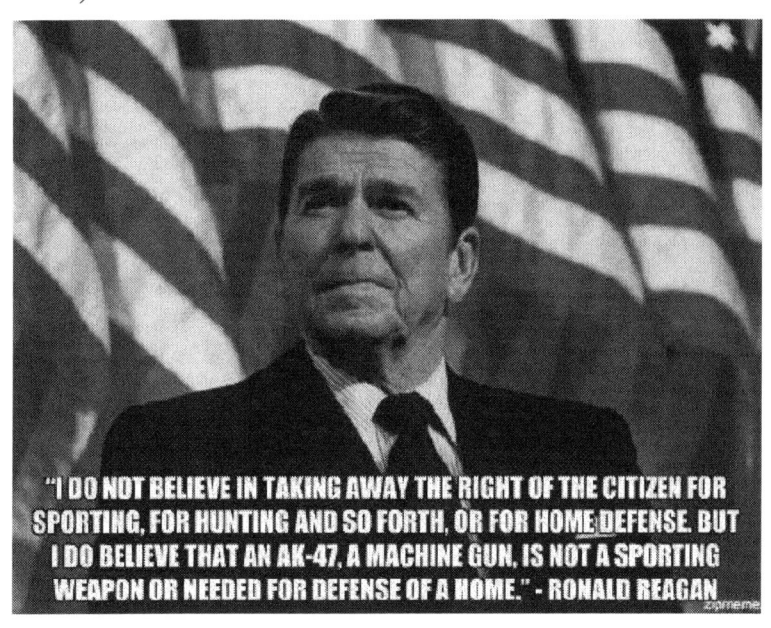

> "I DO NOT BELIEVE IN TAKING AWAY THE RIGHT OF THE CITIZEN FOR SPORTING, FOR HUNTING AND SO FORTH, OR FOR HOME DEFENSE. BUT I DO BELIEVE THAT AN AK-47, A MACHINE GUN, IS NOT A SPORTING WEAPON OR NEEDED FOR DEFENSE OF A HOME." - RONALD REAGAN

- **Lawsuits against gun manufacturers**: Thanks to the 2005 Protection of Lawful Commerce in Arms Act (PLCAA), the gun industry is the only one in America that enjoys 100% total legal immunity from any liability. Victims' families who even *attempt* to file suit for negligent sales or faulty design are dismissed, slapped with countersuits and even forced to pay gun manufacturers' legal fees.

*But wait, hang on! You can't sue General Motors if you get hit by a car! Why should you be able to sue gun makers?*

The reason we have seat belts, air bags, shatter-resistant glass, child car seats, mirrors, anti-lock brakes and so on is BECAUSE the auto manufacturers have a legal obligation to make sure their products as safe as possible. Because we have federal safety standards and regulations for cars, and federal regulation of automobile sales. Because we understand that studying motor vehicles, traffic patterns, accidents and suicides leads to better, safer products in the hands of the public. Because the Seventh Amendment guarantees the right to bring civil claims before a judge and/or jury.

> **Imagine 300,000,000 cars.**
> No speed limits.
> No registration.
> No drivers licenses.
> No training.
> **Replace cars with guns.**
> That's what we've got.
>
> One Million Moms and Dads Against Gun Violence

Tobacco, auto and alcohol companies have long been held legally responsible for the way they market their products and to whom. But, thanks to the PLCAA, gun manufacturers can market as violently and irresponsibly as they want, even to minors.

Wouldn't it be cool if all guns had built-in safety features that prevented "accidental discharges," or use by a non-registered owner, or mass shootings? Too bad that's just science fiction...right?

- **Smart guns** are not the future – they're already here. Also called "personalized firearms," smart guns use voice and/or fingerprint recognition, radio-frequency ID, mechanical locks, magnetic rings and other safety features that allow it to function only when operated by the registered user(s). This means fewer "accidents," thefts, misuse and suicides. "Smart" technology also works for trigger locks and safes.

Alas, you can't have any of them because the folks at the NRA don't like them. They claim smart guns have a failure rate of up to 40%, despite no other testing laboratory finding any with a failure rate above one percent. Also they are very worried that "a criminal, a hacker or even a government agency could turn your gun on or off anytime they wanted." And they condone threats and attacks directed at gun sellers who carry smart gun technology, so that dealers are scared to sell them.

And on top of all that, they also lie about their own opposition to smart guns.

After each highly-publicized shooting, the NRA responds with lies and paranoia, pushing its agenda of more guns for everyone, everywhere. "They're coming to take your guns!" they cry, like stupid inbred hounds.

And gun sales skyrocket.

And the gun companies get rich, and the NRA gets a generous slice, and more people die.

And round and round it goes.

*Cycle diagram:*
- NRA stokes fear and paranoia ("They're comin' fer yer gunz! Bad Guyz everywhere!")
- More gun sales $$$$$$
- More guns in the wrong hands
- More people get shot

CHAPTER 14

# *But what about the RESEARCH?!*

*"More guns lead to less crime. Guns are used more in self-defense than in criminal acts. Mass shootings only happen in 'gun-free zones.' Good Guys with Guns can stop crime in action. Guns make women safer."*

The gun lobby has shouted and whispered these lies for decades, until they become accepted as fact. All of them come from a single source; John Lott, whose pinched little talking head may be seen on every cable news show after every publicized shooting.

There's no disputing the fact that Lott is highly intelligent. He's held positions at Ivy League universities and the University of Chicago, where he published his groundbreaking book, *More Guns, Less Crime*. It's remained "the Bible of the gun lobby" ever since, no matter how many times it gets debunked. And over the last 20 years, Lott's book of fairy tales has had the shit debunked out of it.

Like his claim that, in 98% of defensive gun uses, all a law-abiding Good Guy has to do is brandish a gun in self-defense. And 98% of the time, the Bad Guy slinks away in terror at the mere *sight* of an armed citizen ready to defend him/herself.

> John Lott is a UCLA-trained economist who used to have a real career as a reputable researcher before he got nailed for faking his research. But don't worry – things turned out fine! These days he draws a big fat paycheck from the gun lobby as their go-to lackey for "facts," "statistics," and other "evidence" which is clearly reverse-engineered to yield the results his bosses want. He may be a liar, but he's far from stupid.

Wait, what?

No other credible research anywhere, by anyone, comes close to the same findings. In fact, all evidence points consistently to the opposite conclusion: the presence of a gun *increases* the odds that the situation will <u>escalate to violence</u>. How do you even collect data on these instances anyway, if there's no police report? If the mere sight of a gun were enough to protect you, why carry it loaded? Why carry a real gun at all? Buy a toy gun, carve one out of soap, or carry a gun-shaped phone case. If a highly trained sharpshooter can't always stop a mass shooter right away, why would an ordinary civilian do any better? Plus, do we all really have to walk around all the time constantly ready for battle?

In fact, all of Lott's "research" focuses on the relationship between guns and crime…and guess what? Turns out the Harvard Injury Control Research Center is wrong! So are the National Academy of Sciences and Johns Hopkins and the National Bureau of Economic Research and Yale and Valparaiso University Law Review and the journal Science, and the *only* person who is right is John Lott.

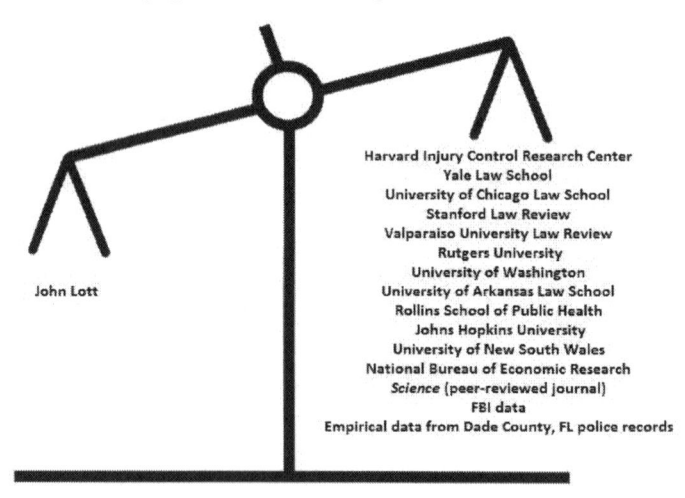

*How the gun lobby sees things*

Even the gun lobby's other pet researchers don't agree with Lott's methods; on the other hand, no one's exactly winning Nobel prizes in the field of gunhumper studies. Gary Kleck and Marc Gertz, for example, have "estimated" - based on a single telephone survey of 5,000 Florida households - that there are between 800,000 and 2.5 million defensive gun uses in America every year. The actual number reported by the FBI, is nearly *10,000 times lower*: of the 11,622 gun homicides committed in 2012, only 259 were found to be justifiable self-defense by a private citizen (e.g., not an off-duty police officer).

But hey, anybody can be off by a factor of ten thousand, right?

Both Lott's methodology and his integrity came under serious scrutiny in 2003, when he was a resident scholar at the conservative American Enterprise Institute, and the other researchers were total dicks to him about not being able to replicate his results and wanting to see the data behind his claims...which had been lost in a hard drive crash, gosh darn it. Also he moved and lost the tally sheets from his data, and he just can't remember the names of the other students involved in the research. Anyway, any flaws in his model were just innocent coding errors, but really there were no coding errors, well ok, there were, but they didn't end up affecting the results IN ANY WAY.

It's hard to stick to your guns amid this kind of bullying and overwhelming proof of "research fraud" and "cooked data," but Lott has developed a thick skin against both criticism and facts. He's also been caught using caught using a fake sock puppet persona to defend his work, and publishing "rebuttals" to his critics under the names of his colleagues, or creates fake identities to praise his own work.

> "[Lott's book] is one of the best crafted arguments for a particular position I have ever read," said firearms safety researcher Arthur Kellermann...right before adding that it is "highly selective, and therefore misleading. I am surprised that...he didn't bother to talk to at least one mainstream criminologist, policy analyst, physician or public health researcher."

Researchers at Harvard have conducted numerous studies comparing data across states and countries with wildly different gun laws and concluded, quite simply, "Where there are more guns, there is more homicide."

David Hemenway, Director of the Harvard Injury Control Research Center, says "virtually all of Lott's analyses are faulty; his findings are not 'facts' but are erroneous."

"Lott's research was…very instrumental over decades in having more states pass laws to make it easier to get permits to carry concealed loaded guns, and to lessen the barriers for those permit holders to take guns in ever more places," says Daniel Webster, the director of the Johns Hopkins Center for Gun Policy and Research. There's just one problem: "It's all based upon Lott's scholarship that has been completely discredited."

**The critics rave about John Lott:**

When even crazy-ass Michelle Malkin says Lott has an "extensive willingness to deceive to protect and promote his work," you know it's bad.

Researchers at Johns Hopkins University reviewed all existing academic literature on right-to-carry, in which "the most consistent finding…is that RTC laws are associated with an increase in aggravated assaults."

The American Law and Economics Review stated in 2011 that "aggravated assault rises when RTC laws are adopted," and that "the conclusion…that RTC laws reduce murder has no statistical support."

> A 2004 review of Lott's work by the National Academy of Sciences concluded there was "no credible evidence that the passage of right-to-carry laws decreases or increases violent crime."

ArmedWithReason.com details every single methodological flaw in Lott's work: he often claims cause-and-effect without support, and has been proven to skew results with clever tricks like omitting tables or failing to include the entire state of Florida in his data. He has been known to alter his online content after criticism, then gaslights his critics about these alterations. There are plenty of other researchers who have definitively disproven Lott's findings well beyond the reasonable doubt of scholarly dissent.

> Fred Rivara, epidemiologist at the University of Washington: "There is no data supporting his argument that the further arming of citizens will lessen the death toll in massacres like the one this week in Connecticut. There are in fact rigorous scientific data showing that having a gun in the home INCREASES the risk of violent death in the home." Even despite the Dickey-Wicker Amendment prohibiting federal funding for gun violence research, "... there is more than enough research out there to conclude beyond a reasonable doubt that more guns lead to more violence."

Whatever Lott lacks in scholarly integrity, he makes up for in rhetorical brilliance. Watch him sometime, dodging questions and throwing out shaky statistics like a ninja warrior. He refutes his many critics with Kafkaesque obfuscations and cries of conspiracies. He's a master at leading his opponents down a winding labyrinth of arguments "so complex that only other highly trained regression analysts can understand, let alone refute, them."

But it doesn't matter to the gunlickers. All they care about is that Lott's "work" scratches an itch for them. It confirms what they already believe on an emotional level: that guns equal power, and power equals safety, that there are simple solutions to complex issues and that you can solve problems by shooting at them.

> <u>Daniel Webster</u>, Director of the Johns Hopkins Center for Gun Policy and Research: "It does not appear to be the case that there is any beneficial effect [to concealed carry]. So if you want to argue that the reason we have so many mass shootings, the reason that the United States has a homicide rate about seven times higher than other developed countries, is because we don't allow enough concealed carry of firearms, the data just don't bear that out. And the thought experiment that you do is almost laughable."
>
> **Almost!**

> **Fun fact!** Gary Kleck, the same guy who "extrapolated" 2,500,000 from 5,000, once accused the director of the Harvard Injury Control Research Center of being "untrained in survey methods."

CHAPTER 15

# *Violent crime/mass shootings only happen in gun-free zones!*

This is one of the NRA's favorites, and it's truly amazing how fiercely this belief hangs on when it's so easy to disprove:

- An independent investigation of 83 mass shootings between 1982-2016 found zero evidence that any of the shooters chose their location based on firearms policies in that area.

- Between one-half and two-thirds of all mass shooters either take their own lives at the end of their spree or commit "suicide by cop." They generally don't intend to survive, so the possibility of armed citizens (or law enforcement) does not deter them.

- Many of the "armed citizens" who save the day are trained law enforcement and/or military, not fat drunk idiots who happened to be standing in the snack aisle when ISIS attacked the Piggly Wiggly.

- Defining "gun-free zones" is tricky, though many of what the NRA claims are "gun-free zones" actually DID have armed people present: the Washington Navy Yard, Pulse nightclub in Orlando, Umpqua Community College, the Sikh temple in Oakland, Wisconsin, the Tyler, Texas courthouse shooting, the massacre of police officers in Dallas, and the list goes on.

- Would-be Good Guys have a far better chance of ending up dead than of saving the day. If the Bad Guys don't kill them first, the other armed-citizen Good Guys just might. In active shooter situations, it's impossible for police to distinguish between Good Guys and Bad Guys. All they're looking for is someone with a gun, and armed vigilantes only make their job harder.

It's not that legitimate defensive gun uses *never* happen – they do. But they're dwarfed by "accidental discharges," and vanish into nothingness against the tens of thousands of murders and suicides

> "So many people have told me to my face, 'If I was there with you that day, I would have saved the lives of students all around you.' That almost offends me."
>
> *The class was slow to realize what was happening. They attributed the bangs they heard from the hallway to construction noise.*
>
> "When I felt the force of that bullet, when I felt the blood, when I smelled the propellant, that's when I realized this guy's killing people. You don't think rationally. "You don't understand what's going on – it's absolutely terrifying and crazy."
>
> --Virginia Tech survivor Colin Goddard

### How many mass shootings have there been?

No one seems to be sure; estimates and definitions vary. An FBI study of 160 mass shootings found that a grand total of 5 were stopped by armed bystanders.

The FBI defines mass shootings as 4 or more fatalities, NOT including the shooter. The above map uses 3 as the magic number of corpses. Different research uses different standards, and it gets hard to keep track of. That's by design. But the very fact that we have too many to keep accurate track of is sickening. And they're on the rise.

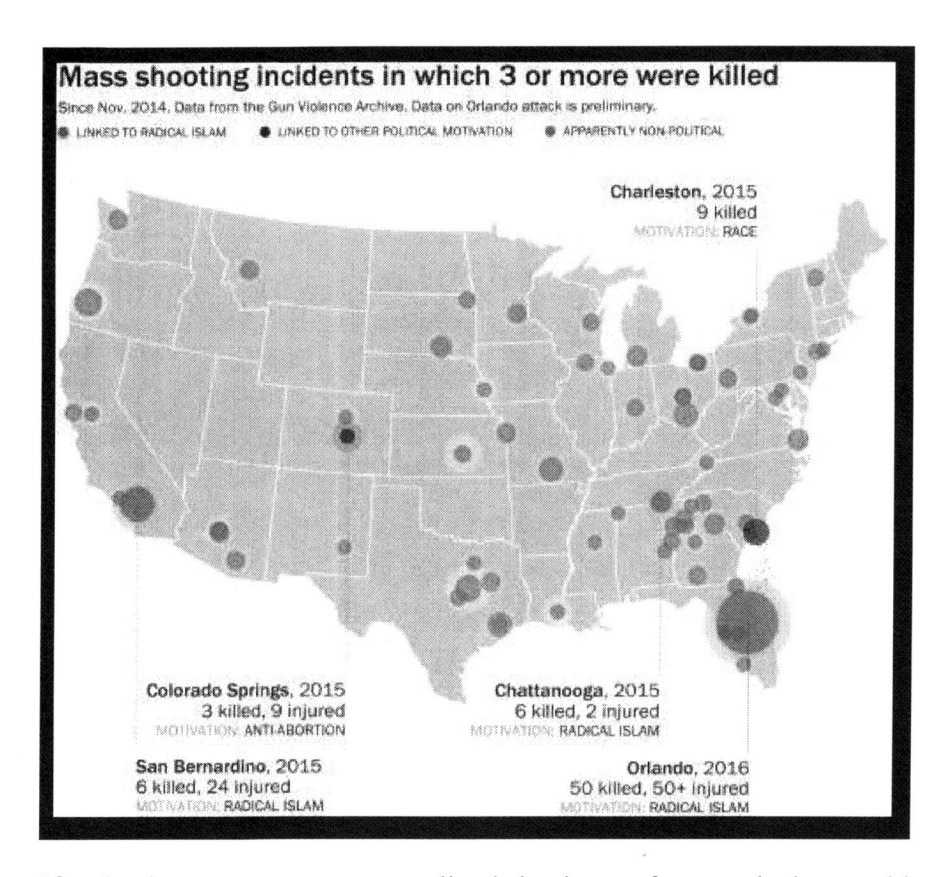

**Mass shooting incidents in which 3 or more were killed**
Since Nov. 2014. Data from the Gun Violence Archive. Data on Orlando attack is preliminary.
● LINKED TO RADICAL ISLAM   ● LINKED TO OTHER POLITICAL MOTIVATION   ● APPARENTLY NON-POLITICAL

Charleston, 2015
9 killed
MOTIVATION: RACE

Colorado Springs, 2015
3 killed, 9 injured
MOTIVATION: ANTI-ABORTION

Chattanooga, 2015
6 killed, 2 injured
MOTIVATION: RADICAL ISLAM

San Bernardino, 2015
6 killed, 24 injured
MOTIVATION: RADICAL ISLAM

Orlando, 2016
50 killed, 50+ injured
MOTIVATION: RADICAL ISLAM

If only there were some centralized database of research that could prevent the next mass slaughter. But that would be tyranny, JUST LIKE HITLER.

## CHAPTER 16

## *"Hitler took the guns!"*

Unlike the vast majority of the NRA's claims, this one is only 99% pure horseshit. The answer's a bit complicated, so my tl;dr version is usually "No he didn't, you gunlicking fuckwit." But in case you want to go into more detail, here it is:

> **Fun Fact!**
>
> Germany had its own problem with school shootings in the early 2000s, which they solved by passing tighter gun control laws.

Under the strict laws of the Weimar Republic, all private gun ownership was banned in Germany between 1920-28. But, as you might imagine, there were plenty of firearms already in private hands after the first World War. Later the ban was eased – somewhat -- with a rigorous permit and licensing process for owning, selling, carrying or manufacturing firearms. All new purchases of firearms were registered – but again, this did not apply to the majority of guns in private hands at the time.

When the Nazis came to power, one of the first things they did was to roll back many of these laws: deregulating sales of arms and ammunition, making handguns easier to own, extending permit periods, and making guns available to children under 18. The bottom line is that it was far easier for the average German citizen to own a gun during the Third Reich than at any time before or since.

With one exception, of course. A 1938 law forbade Jews from owning weapons of any kind. The Nazis did use the state gun registry files to seize firearms from their political enemies. But, as with radios, bicycles and other prohibited items, "many Jews possessed guns" in spite of these laws.

> "The availability of guns was not a pivotal issue in Hitler's rise to power."

But how exactly would ordinary Jewish civilians have defeated the Third Reich with guns? What good is a gun during an SS strike or an air raid? Even if every civilian had an AK-47…even ten AK-47s each…it's not like they would have stopped the tanks from rolling into Poland, France, the Netherlands, North Africa. That's just not how global conflict works.

**Ted Nugent blames Jews for gun control in Facebook posts**

*This is an NRA board member, in case you forgot.*

The SS and other high-ranking Nazi officers also had gun boners rivalling those of any American redneck. They collected and exchanged pistols as ceremonial gifts, presented them as awards, and probably all sat around together in the bunker stroking them and fondling them and oiling them up. Well, they were *very* sexy guns:

*The Walther PPK, preferred gun of James Bond (who the gun nuts imagine themselves as) and der Fuehrer (who they actually have more in common with).*

## CHAPTER 17

# *Muslims, mental illness, and other misdirections*

How many times have you heard *"It's not a gun problem – the problem is __________________!"*

You can fill in this blank with pretty much anything: Muslims, foreigners, terrorists, gangs, violent video games and media, secularism, broken homes, toxic masculinity, feminism, race war, Democrats, gun control, whatever. Just don't blame guns, nope, definitely not the guns in any way at all.

- Muslims: Despite efforts to depict mass shootings as the work of a specific religious or ethnic group, the evidence is clear:

**Blue = Muslim shooters** **Red = non-Muslim shooters**

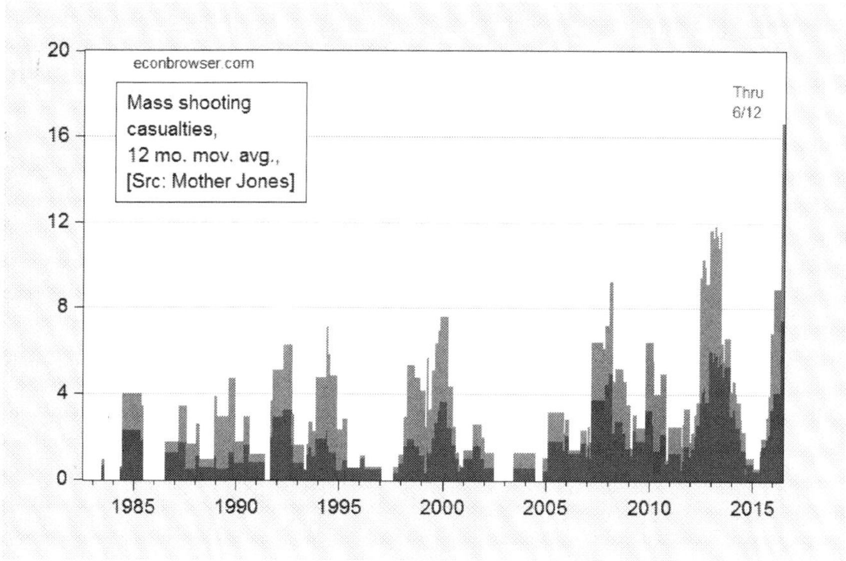

econbrowser.com
Mass shooting casualties, 12 mo. mov. avg., [Src: Mother Jones]
Thru 6/12
20
16
12
8
4
0
1985
1990
1995
2000
2005
2010
2015

- Foreigners and/or terrorists: Domestic right-wing terror attacks happen nearly twice as frequently as violent jihadist attacks. If you count the Orlando nightclub shooting (as investigators do), then domestic terror attacks have also killed twice as any people than jihadism since September 11, 2001.

- Gangs: You'll see bullshit statistics from the gunhuggers claiming that 50% or 85% or 147% of gun violence is gang-related, and therefore doesn't count. There's a difference between "Most gun homicides are gang-related" (false) and "Most gang homicides involve a gun" (true). Plus, what the fuck is "It's just gang violence" even supposed to mean? I heard all lives matter.

- Violent entertainment: Just no. We've studied this and studied this, and there is just no meaningful correlation between media violence and societal violence. See also: Japan. Their horror films are *incredibly* violent, as is some truly upsetting gore anime and manga. In 2014, Japan had a total of six gun deaths.

- Mental health: Everybody's favorite scapegoat. BONUS: It even makes you sound as if you give a shit about the mentally ill, even if you vote to cut mental health services! If only we could just address mental health, maybe we can continue to ignore the other 95% of shootings where the perpetrators have no record of mental illness.

Statistically, mass shooters are most likely to be conservative young white guys who can't get laid. But these also exist in other countries, along with everything else listed above. The U.S., however, has one additional thing these other countries don't: insanely easy access to guns by anybody, anywhere.

# CHAPTER 18

# *"Most gun owners are law-abiding; it's not fair to punish them all for the actions of a few!"*

That first sentence is true. Here are some sentences that are also true:

- Most people don't commit rape or robbery.
- Relatively few people drink and drive.
- Several million people did not embezzle from their employers yesterday.

Do we give these folks medals and just shrug off the ones who aren't abiding by these basic expectations?

We're not worried about the ones who *don't* shoot people for playing loud music, throwing popcorn, talking back to men, cutting them off in traffic, putting clamato in beer, and other deadly threats. We need to address the ones who DO. Every single mass shooter was once a law-abiding gun owner…until the moment they weren't.

Responsible gun owners favor tighter gun regulations by a wide margin. Responsible gun owners don't feel the need to keep loaded firearms at the ready in their shower, couch, laundry hamper, toilet tank, in the drywall, in cereal boxes and their child's nursery. (None of those are made up.)

Responsible gun owners know the NRA stopped representing them a long time ago. What will help tremendously is for more responsible gun owners to step up and make themselves heard over the gun lobby.

CHAPTER 19

## *"There's nothing we can do."*

**What you can do:**

Speak out against easy access to guns. Ask if there are guns in homes where your kids play. Call, email, write and tweet your state and national legislators to tell them you want legislation to close background check loopholes and keep guns out of the hands of dangerous people. Put gun sense bumper stickers on your car. Vote for candidates who will stand up to the NRA. Join an organization that works to reform gun laws, including but not limited to:

> **Pro tip:** Congressbeings and Senators pay the most attention to phone calls. They really do keep count of them every day, and you know the NRA folks are ringing their phones off the hook. Find your representative here and give em a call to urge them to support gun law reform OR to thank them for the support they're already giving.
>
> This is especially important in red states.

American Coalition for Responsible Gun Ownership: originally started by a Facebook group by musician and firearms enthusiast Mark Carman, works to promote safety and responsibility among gun owners. He could really use your help.

Americans for Responsible Solutions: Founded by former AZ Congresswoman Gabby Giffords and her husband, astronaut Mark Kelly, after Gabby was shot in the head during a mass shooting in Tucson on January 8, 2011. Focuses mainly on lobbying federal legislators and supporting candidates who work for gun law reform.

Brady Campaign to Prevent Gun Violence: Founded after press secretary Jim Brady was shot while protecting President Reagan from a would-be assassin, the Brady Campaign lobbies for effective gun legislation and battles the NRA in court as necessary, and it's necessary a lot. Also organizes the annual Million Mom March.

Coalition to Stop Gun Violence: Senator Chris Murphy (D-CT) credits the CSGV with "lead[ing] the way in exposing the dangerous insurrectionist ideology promoted by the NRA."

Everytown for Gun Safety: Umbrella organization for Mayors Against Illegal Guns, Moms Demand Action and the Everytown Survivor Network. Conducts independent research on the state of gun violence in America.

Gun Owners for Responsible Ownership: Founded in response to the December, 2012 shooting at the Clackamas Town Center in suburban Portland, Oregon, GORGO supports laws requiring complete background checks for all gun purchases and the secure storage of guns away from children.

Moms Demand Action: The national grassroots movement started the day after the massacre at Sandy Hook Elementary School in 2012. Partnered with Everytown in 2014 as a kind of "hearts and minds" recruitment campaign for work on the ground (phone banking, canvassing, meeting with legislators).

Sandy Hook Promise: Works to "protect children from gun violence by encouraging and supporting solutions that create safer, healthier homes, schools and communities."

And of course...

The Betsy Riot: Fucks shit up.

#betsyriot

#fuckyourguns

# *Bibliography*

Introduction:

1. never going to happen: Gun Violence Archive, "Mass Shootings." 2016. http://www.shootingtracker.com/

2. all the U.S. wars since the Revolution: PolitiFact, "More Americans killed by guns since 1968 than in all U.S. wars, columnist Nicholas Kristof writes." Aug. 27, 2015. http://www.politifact.com/punditfact/statements/2015/aug/27/nicholas-kristof/more-americans-killed-guns-1968-all-wars-says-colu/

3. millions of law-abiding gun owners: Politifact, "Most NRA Members Back Background Checks on All Gun Purchases." Mar. 18, 2015. http://www.politifact.com/wisconsin/statements/2015/mar/18/lena-taylor/most-nra-members-back-background-checks-all-gun-pu/

4. loophole-free background checks: UC Davis Health System, "Inside Gun Shows: What Goes on when Everybody Thinks Nobody's Watching." 2009. http://www.ucdmc.ucdavis.edu/welcome/features/20090923_gun_study/

5. state licensing of gun dealers: Law Center to Prevent Gun Violence, "Dealer Regulations." 2016. http://smartgunlaws.org/gun-laws/policy-areas/gun-dealer-sales/dealer-regulations/#state

6. people who are a danger to themselves or others: Politifact, "Schumer: 244 People on Terror Watch List Tried to Buy Guns in 2015; 91% Got Them." June 15, 2016. http://www.politifact.com/truth-o-meter/statements/2016/jun/15/charles-schumer/charles-schumer-terror-watch-list-buy-guns-got-the/

7. cut through the bullshit: American Psychological Association, "Speaking of Psychology: Dispelling the Myth of Violence and Mental Illness." Episode 27. http://www.apa.org/research/action/speaking-of-psychology/dispelling-myth.aspx

8. number-one killer: CNN.com, "Look to MADD in Changing Our Gun Culture." Dec. 16, 2012. http://www.cnn.com/2012/12/24/opinion/lightner-madd-effect/

9. letters to newspapers: The New York Times, "Long Island Opinion; Drinking and Driving Can Mix." June 3, 1984. http://www.nytimes.com/1984/06/03/nyregion/long-island-opinion-drinking-and-driving-can-mix.html?smid=tw-share

10. tens of thousands: LifeSafer, "The History of Drunk Driving Laws in the U.S." Jan. 22, 2013. https://www.lifesafer.com/blog/the-history-of-drunk-driving-laws-in-the-u-s/

11. by 50%: MADD.org, "Drunk Driving Statistics." 2016.

12. does not appear: Huffington Post, "Gun Control Debate: A View from Hoplophiliaville." Oct. 12, 2015. http://www.huffingtonpost.com/warren-j-blumenfeld/gun-control-debate-a-view_b_8274902.html

13. Jason Brennan: Quartz.com, "An Ethicist Explains What Brexit Voters Forgot on Their Way to the Polls." June 27, 2016. http://qz.com/717022/an-ethicist-explains-what-brexit-voters-forgot-on-their-way-to-the-polls/

14. the weapons effect: Psychology Today, "The Weapons Effect." Jan. 18, 2013. https://www.psychologytoday.com/blog/get-psyched/201301/the-weapons-effect

15. overwhelming majority: Fivethirtyeight.com, "Most Americans Agree with Obama that More Guns Buyers Should Get Background Checks." Jan. 5, 2016. http://fivethirtyeight.com/features/most-americans-agree-with-obama-that-more-gun-buyers-should-get-background-checks/

*Ch. 1:*

1. <u>300 million</u>: The University of Sydney, "Compare the United States." 2016. http://www.gunpolicy.org/firearms/compare/194/number_of_privately_owned_firearms

2. <u>firearms research summary</u>: Harvard Injury Control Center, 2016. https://www.hsph.harvard.edu/hicrc/firearms-research/overall/

3. <u>National Institutes of Health</u>: American Journal of Medicine, "Violent Death Rates: The U.S. Compared with OECD Countries, 2010." Mar. 2016. https://www.ncbi.nlm.nih.gov/pubmed/26551975

4. <u>credible research</u>: Harvard Injury Control Center, "Homicide." 2016. https://www.hsph.harvard.edu/hicrc/firearms-research/guns-and-death/

*Ch. 2:*

1. <u>highest rate</u>: The Washington Post, "Gun Ownership in the U.S.: A Primer." Dec. 7, 2015. https://www.washingtonpost.com/news/in-theory/wp/2015/12/07/gun-ownership-in-the-u-s-a-primer/?tid=a_inl&utm_term=.0da8cdbc9ea8

2. <u>Yemen</u>: The Blaze, "How Many People Own Guns in America?" Mar. 19, 2013. http://www.theblaze.com/stories/2013/03/19/how-many-people-own-guns-in-america-and-is-gun-ownership-actually-declining/

3. <u>1 in 3</u>: NPR, "Guns in America, By the Numbers." Jan. 5, 2016. http://www.npr.org/2016/01/05/462017461/guns-in-america-by-the-numbers

4. <u>average of 8</u>: The Washington Post, "The Average Gun Owner Now Owns 8 Guns – Double What It Used to Be." Oct. 21, 2015. https://www.washingtonpost.com/news/wonk/wp/2015/10/21/the-aver

5. <u>radicalized</u>: The Washington Post, "Wisdom from a Gun-Owning Moderate." Sept. 25, 2015. https://www.washingtonpost.com/opinions/wisdom-from-a-gun-owning-moderate/2015/09/25/05f1e6b0-5256-11e5-9812-92d5948a40f8_story.html?utm_term=.c832ab691e7f

6. <u>does not</u>: Law Center to Prevent Gun Violence, "Canada." 2016. http://www.gunpolicy.org/firearms/region/canada

7. <u>All evidence</u>: Library of Congress, "Firearms-Control Legislation and Policy – Australia." 2016. https://www.loc.gov/law/help/firearms-control/australia.php#Statistical

8. <u>an astonishing 80%</u>: Institute for the Study of Labor (Bonn), "Do Gun Buyback Save Lives?" June 2010. http://ftp.iza.org/dp4995.pdf

9. <u>zero mass shootings</u>:

10. <u>4 gun homicides and 78 gun suicides</u>: ScienceAlert, "Massive Study of Australia's Gun Laws Shows One Thing: They Work." June 23, 2016. http://www.sciencealert.com/20-year-review-of-australia-s-gun-laws-has-one-clear-finding-they-work

11. <u>2 gun homicides and 12 gun suicides</u>: LVPGV, "Scotland." 2016. http://www.gunpolicy.org/firearms/region/scotland

12. <u>overwhelming majority</u>: BBC News, "Why British Police Don't Have Guns." Sept. 19, 2012. http://www.bbc.com/news/magazine-19641398

13. <u>total of 4 gun homicides and 4 gun suicides</u>: LCPGV, "Northern Ireland." 2016. http://www.gunpolicy.org/firearms/region/northern-ireland

14. <u>Belfast Agreement</u>: Gov.UK, "The Belfast Agreement." Apr. 10, 1998. https://www.gov.uk/government/publications/the-belfast-agreement

15. <u>importers</u>: Graduate Institute of International and Development Studies, Geneva, "Small Arms Survey 2015." http://www.smallarmssurvey.org/fileadmin/docs/A-Yearbook/2015/eng/Small-Arms-Survey-2015-Highlights-EN.pdf

16. <u>strictest gun laws</u>: Asia Pacific Law Review, "Japanese Gun Control." 1993. http://www.guncite.com/journals/dkjgc.html

17. <u>fairly high rates</u>: Library of Congress, "Firearms-Control Legislation and Policy: Japan." 2016. https://www.loc.gov/law/help/firearms-control/japan.php#Law

18. <u>11 firearm homicides and 15 firearm suicides</u>: LCPGV, "Japan." 2016. http://www.gunpolicy.org/firearms/region/japan

19. <u>sword control</u>: Yale Law Journal, "Book Review: Goldilocks Apologizes." Vol. 86 1509-1521, 1977. http://web.mit.edu/gtmarx/www/goldilocks.pdf

20. <u>politicizing tragedy</u>: Washington Post, "Paul Ryan Held a Moment of Silence. Then Some House Democrats Held a Protest." June 14, 2016. https://www.washingtonpost.com/news/morning-mix/wp/2016/06/14/paul-ryan-held-a-moment-of-silence-then-some-house-democrats-held-a-protest/

21. <u>1.3 million guns</u>: LCPGV, "Norway." 2016. http://www.gunpolicy.org/firearms/region/norway

22. <u>2009-2013</u>: Rampage Shooting Index, 2013. http://archive.is/f4gbv

23. wound: Arch Daily, ""'Memory Wound' Fractures Landscape, Commemorates Victims of Norway's Massacre." Mar. 6, 2014. http://www.archdaily.com/483695/memory-wound-fractures-landscape-commemorates-victims-of-norway-s-massacre

*Ch. 3:*

1. deadliest Means Matter, "Lethality of Suicide Methods," August 03, 2016 <https://www.hsph.harvard.edu/means-matter/means-matter/case-fatality/>

2. at least 20 states: LCPGV, "2015 Gun Law State Scorecard." http://gunlawscorecard.org/

3. 3 miles: Rawstory, "OK Gun Range Owner Insists Howitzer Fired Safely After Shell Blasts House 3 Miles Away." June 26, 2014. http://www.rawstory.com/2014/06/ok-gun-range-owner-insists-howitzer-fired-safely-after-shell-blasts-house-3-miles-away/

4. FBI Crime Statistics: FBI.UCR, "2014 Expanded Homicide Data." https://ucr.fbi.gov/crime-in-the-u.s/2014/crime-in-the-u.s.-2014/tables/expanded-homicide-data/expanded_homicide_data_table_8_murder_victims_by_weapon_2010-2014.xls

*Ch. 4:*

1. accidental drownings: Centers for Disease Control and Prevention, "Unintentional Drowning – Get the Facts." Apr. 28, 2016. http://www.cdc.gov/homeandrecreationalsafety/water-safety/waterinjuries-factsheet.html

2. accidental/negligent shootings: National Vital Statistics Reports, "Deaths: Final Tally for 2013." Feb. 16, 2016. http://www.cdc.gov/nchs/data/nvsr/nvsr64/nvsr64_02.pdf

3. kills more people: CDC, "Leading Causes of Death." Oct. 7, 2016. http://www.cdc.gov/nchs/fastats/leading-causes-of-death.htm

*Ch. 5:*

1. the evidence: CDC, "Firearms Mortality by State: 2014." Feb. 3, 2016. http://www.cdc.gov/nchs/pressroom/sosmap/firearm_mortality/firearm.htm

**2. 2013 gun ownership**: Injury Prevention, "Gun Ownership and Social Gun Culture." June 29, 2015. http://injuryprevention.bmj.com/content/early/2015/06/09/injuryprev-2015-041586.full.pdf

3. more gun deaths: Mother Jones, "10 Pro-Gun Myths, Shot Down." Jan. 31, 2015. http://www.motherjones.com/politics/2013/01/pro-gun-myths-fact-check

4. expanded state scorecard: The Brady Campaign State Scorecard, March 2015. http://crimadvisor.com/data/Brady-State-Scorecard-2014.pdf

5. Brady Campaign: LCPGV, "2013 State Scorecard: Why Gun Laws Matter." http://www.bradycampaign.org/sites/default/files/SCGLM-Final10-spreads-points.pdf

*Ch. 6:*

1. nowhere near: Pew Research Center, "Despite Recent Shootings, Chicago Nowhere Near U.S. 'Murder Capital.'" July 14, 2014. http://www.pewresearch.org/fact-tank/2014/07/14/despite-recent-shootings-chicago-nowhere-near-u-s-murder-capital/

2. 2014 FBI crime statistics: Chicago CBS Local, "FBI's Violent Crime Statistics for Every City in America." Oct. 22, 2015. http://chicago.cbslocal.com/2015/10/22/violent-crime-statistics-for-every-city-in-america/

3. <u>2006-07 and 2009-10</u>: CDC Mortality and Morbidity Weekly Report, "Firearm Homicides and Suicides in Major Metropolitan Areas." August 2, 2013. http://www.cdc.gov/mmwr/pdf/wk/mm6230.pdf

4. <u>specific areas</u>: Chicago Tribune, "Chicago's Shooting Victims." Nov. 20, 2016. http://crime.chicagotribune.com/chicago/shootings/

5. *Obama's Chicago*: The Washington Post, "Gun Control Opponents Love to Cite Chicago. So How Does it Compare to the Rest of America?" Oct. 5, 2015. https://www.washingtonpost.com/news/the-fix/wp/2015/10/05/gun-control-opponents-love-to-cite-chicago-so-how-does-it-compare-to-the-rest-of-america/

6. <u>overturned or gutted</u>: Chicago Tribune, "Chicago's Gun Laws Not as Strict as GOP Candidates Claim." Oct. 8, 2015. http://www.chicagotribune.com/news/local/breaking/ct-chicago-gun-laws-not-as-strict-as-gop-candidates-claim-20151008-story.html

7. <u>Indiana</u>: FOX 59, "Statistics Rank Indiana Low in Gun Violence Prevention." June 23, 2016. http://fox59.com/2016/06/23/statistics-rank-indiana-low-in-gun-violence-prevention/

8. <u>street gangs</u>: Indy Star, "Indiana Gun Show Customer Sold to Chicago Gangs." May 16, 2014. http://www.indystar.com/story/news/crime/2014/05/16/indiana-gun-show-customer-sold-chicago-gangs/9163587/

9. "<u>bad apple</u>": Brady Campaign, "The Truth About Gun Dealers in America." 2015. https://www.bradycampaign.org/sites/default/files/TheTruthAboutGunDealersInAmerica.pdf

10. state licensing: Chicago Now, "Why Illinois Needs HB1016, the Gun Dealer Licensing Act, and What You Can Do to Make Sure We Get It." May 25, 2016. http://www.chicagonow.com/reflections-chicago-life/2016/05/why-illinois-needs-hb1016-the-gun-dealer-licensing-act-and-what-you-can-do-to-make-sure-we-get-it/

11. How guns get to where they shouldn't be: The New York Times, "How Gun Traffickers Get Around State Laws." Nov. 13, 2015. http://www.nytimes.com/interactive/2015/11/12/us/gun-traffickers-smuggling-state-gun-laws.html?_r=1

*Ch. 8:*

1. "defending gun rights": The New York Times, "Sheriffs Refuse to Enforce Laws on Gun Control." Dec. 15, 2013. http://www.nytimes.com/2013/12/16/us/sheriffs-refuse-to-enforce-laws-on-gun-control.html?_r=0

2. Americans for Gun Safety: AGS, "The Enforcement Gap: Federal Laws Ignored." May 2003. http://content.thirdway.org/publications/10/AGS_Report_-_The_Enforcement_Gap_-_Federal_Gun_Laws_Ignored.pdf

3. wasn't that great: CNN Politics, "Why Even the Gun Laws that Exist Don't Always Get Enforced." Jan. 9, 2016. http://www.cnn.com/2016/01/09/politics/obama-executive-orders-gun-control-enforcement-gap/

4. even presidents: Politico, "Few Chances for GOP to Stop Obama on Guns." Jan. 5, 2016. http://www.politico.com/story/2016/01/gop-congress-block-barack-obama-gun-control-217367

5. opposition and threats: Boston Globe, "AG Faces Sexist, Anti-Gay Slurs After Imposing Gun Ban." July 30, 2016. http://www.bostonglobe.com/metro/2016/07/30/faces-sexist-antigay-slurs-after-imposing-gun-

ban/5yz8YB5iI8JdpnEGqDw7bN/story.html?event=event25

6. Nearly half the U. S.: Yale News, "Gun Control Misperceptions: Q&A with Yale Researcher Benjamin Miller." Jan. 27, 2016. http://news.yale.edu/2016/01/27/gun-control-misperceptions-qa-yale-researcher-benjamin-miller

7. Massachusetts: LCPGV, "Massachusetts." 2015. http://smartgunlaws.org/gun-laws/state-law/massachusetts/

8. Brady Background Check: Brady Campaign, "Background Checks." 2016. http://www.bradycampaign.org/our-impact/campaigns/background-checks

9. "gun show loophole": UCLA Law Review, "Heller's Catch-22." Vol, 56, 2009. http://www.uclalawreview.org/pdf/56-5-13.pdf

10. "Bullshit": Everytown for Gun Safety, "Gun Show Undercover Investigation Videos." Oct. 6, 2009. https://everytownresearch.org/gun-show-undercover-investigation-videos/

11. explanation: Politifact, "3 Things to Know About the 'Gun Show Loophole.'" Jan. 7, 2016. http://www.politifact.com/truth-o-meter/article/2016/jan/07/politifact-sheet-3-things-know-about-gun-show-loop/

*Ch. 9:*

1. colonial gun laws: Mother Jones, "The Second Amendment Doesn't Say What You Think it Does." June 19. 2014. http://www.motherjones.com/politics/2014/06/second-amendment-guns-michael-waldman

2. Catholics: The Volokh Conspiracy, "Laws About Gun Ownership in Early America." Dec. 9, 2011. http://volokh.com/2011/12/09/laws-about-gun-ownership-in-early-america/

3. <u>1792 federal law</u>: The Atlantic, "The Secret History of Guns." Sept. 2011. http://www.theatlantic.com/magazine/archive/2011/09/the-secret-history-of-guns/308608/

4. <u>laid out pretty clearly</u>" The Federalist Papers, "Concerning the Militia." Jan. 10, 1788. https://www.congress.gov/resources/display/content/The+Federalist+Papers#TheFederalistPapers-29

5. <u>bunker-busters</u>: The National Interest, "Meet America's New 'Bunker-Buster' Superbomb." May 20, 2015. http://nationalinterest.org/blog/the-buzz/the-f-35s-new-bunker-buster-super-bomb-12933

6. <u>felony records</u>: Star-Telegram, "Open Carry Activists Not So Open About Criminal Past." Feb. 14, 2015. http://www.star-telegram.com/opinion/opn-columns-blogs/bud-kennedy/article10243031.html

7. <u>Starbucks</u>: Starbucks.com, "An Open Letter from Howard Schultz, CEO." Sept. 17, 2013. https://www.starbucks.com/blog/an-open-letter-from-howard-schultz/1268

## Ch. 10:

1. <u>Shay's Rebellion</u>: George Washington's Mount Vernon, "Shay's Rebellion." 2016. http://www.mountvernon.org/digital-encyclopedia/article/shays-rebellion/

2. <u>but entirely imaginary</u>: The Atlantic, "Constitutional Myth #6: The Second Amendment Allows Citizens to Threaten the Government." June 30, 2011. http://www.theatlantic.com/national/archive/2011/06/constitutional-myth-6-the-second-amendment-allows-citizens-to-threaten-government/241298/

3. <u>this lie</u>: GWMV, "Spurious Quotations." 2016. http://www.mountvernon.org/digital-encyclopedia/article/spurious-quotations/

4. <u>First Annual Address to Congress</u>: GWMV, "First Annual Address to Congress." 2016. http://www.mountvernon.org/digital-encyclopedia/article/first-annual-address-to-congress/

5. <u>fake</u>: Monticello, "Those Who Hammer Their Guns into Ploughshares...." 2016. https://www.monticello.org/site/jefferson/those-who-hammer-their-guns-plowsquotation

6. <u>banning firearms</u>: The University of Virginia Press, "Meeting Minutes of University of Virginia Board of Visitors, 4-5 October, 1824." 2009-2016. http://rotunda.upress.virginia.edu/founders/default.xqy?keys=FOEA-print-04-02-02-4598

7. <u>100% bullshit</u>: Monticello, "Spurious Quotations." 2016. https://www.monticello.org/site/jefferson/spurious-quotations

8. *muzzle-loading muskets and flintlock rifles*: LearnNC.org, "Firing a Musket: 18th-Century Small Arms." Oct. 2008. http://www.learnnc.org/lp/multimedia/9919

9. *26 people in five minutes*: Dept. of Emergency Services and Public Protection, "Sandy Hook Elementary School Shooting Reports." 2013. http://cspsandyhookreport.ct.gov/

10. *U.S. Code Title 18 871*: Legal Information Institute, "Threats Against the President and Successors to the Presidency." https://www.law.cornell.edu/uscode/text/18/871

<u>Ch. 11:</u>

1. <u>Nelson Lund and Adam Winkler</u>: National Constitution Center, "Interactive Constitution: A Common Interpretation of the Second Amendment." Aug. 10, 2016. http://blog.constitutioncenter.org/2016/08/interactive-constitution-a-common-interpretation-of-the-second-amendment/

2. "sovereign citizens": Homeland Security Intelligence Assessment, "Sovereign Citizen Ideology Will Drive Violence at Home, During Travel, and at Government Facilities." Feb. 5, 2015. https://fas.org/irp/eprint/sovereign.pdf

3. insurrectionist theory: The Trace, "Some of Trump's 'Second Amendment People' Already Believe They Have the Right to Fight Tyranny with Guns." Aug. 10, 2016. https://www.thetrace.org/2016/08/donald-trump-gun-rights-2a-insurrectionist-theory/

4. Judge Alex Kozinski: Children of Jewish Holocaust Survivors, "Silveria v. Lockyer: Judge Alex Kozinski's Dissenting Opinion." May 6, 2003. https://cjhsla.org/2013/02/14/silveira-v-lockyer-judge-alex-kozinski%E2%80%99s-dissenting-opinion/

5. *U.S. v. Cruikshank*: FindLaw, "U.S. v. Cruikshank (1875)." http://caselaw.findlaw.com/us-supreme-court/92/542.html

6. *Presser v. Illinois*: Legal Information Institute, Cornell University Law School, "Presser v. Illinois (1886)." https://www.law.cornell.edu/supremecourt/text/116/252

7. *Miller v. Texas*: LII, CULS "Miller v. Texas." May 14, 1894. https://www.law.cornell.edu/supremecourt/text/153/535

8. specific types of firearms: Bureau of Alcohol, Tobacco, Firearms and Explosives, "National Firearms Act." Sept. 22, 2016. https://www.atf.gov/rules-and-regulations/national-firearms-act

9. *D.C. v. Heller*: LII, CULS, "District of Columbia, et al., Petitioners v. Dick Anthony Heller." June 26, 2008. https://www.law.cornell.edu/supct/html/07-290.ZO.html

10. "presumptively lawful": Constitution Center, "The Second Amendment." 2016. http://constitutioncenter.org/interactive-constitution/amendments/amendment-ii

11. *McDonald v Chicago*: IIT Chicago-Kent College of Law, "McDonald v. Chicago." June 28, 2010. https://www.oyez.org/cases/2009/08-1521

12. reversed: LII, CULS, "Bear Arms; Second Amendment." 2016. https://www.law.cornell.edu/anncon/html/amdt2_user.html

*Ch. 12*:

1. "criminal-coddling do-gooders": Perlstein, Rick. *Nixonland: The Rise of a President and the Fracturing of America.* New York: Scribner, 2009. 199. http://tinyurl.com/z5r4wv6

2. National Firearms Act of 1934: Bureau of Alcohol, Tobacco, Firearms and Explosives, "National Firearms Act." Sept. 22, 2016. https://www.atf.gov/rules-and-regulations/national-firearms-act

3. violated any part of the Constitution: Moyers and Company, "The Rise of the NRA." June 12, 2014. http://billmoyers.com/2014/06/12/the-rise-of-the-nra-2/

4. Mabel: Oral Histories of the American South, "Oral History Interview with Mabel Williams. Aug. 20, 1999. http://docsouth.unc.edu/sohp/K-0266/excerpts/excerpt_8789.html

5. Negroes with guns: Williams, Robert F. *Negroes with Guns.* Eastford, CT: Martino Fine Books. 2013. https://www.amazon.com/Negroes-Guns-Robert-F-Williams/dp/1614274118/ref=sr_1_1?ie=UTF8&qid=1472148345&sr=8-1&keywords=negroes+with+guns

6. Franklin L. Orth: *The New Yorker*, "The Birth of the Modern Gun Debate." Apr. 19, 2012. http://www.newyorker.com/books/double-take/the-birth-of-the-modern-gun-debate

7. Richard Harris: The New Yorker, "If You Love Your Guns." Apr. 20, 1968. http://www.newyorker.com/magazine/1968/04/20/if-you-love-your-guns

8. occupation of the California statehouse PBS.org, "State Capitol March." 2002. http://www.pbs.org/hueypnewton/actions/actions_capitolmarch.html

9. "How the NRA's true believers converted a marksmanship group into a mighty gun lobby": Washington Post, Jan. 12, 2013. https://www.washingtonpost.com/politics/how-nras-true-believers-converted-a-marksmanship-group-into-a-mighty-gun-lobby/2013/01/12/51c62288-59b9-11e2-88d0-c4cf65c3ad15_story.html

10. parliamentary procedure: Spitzer, Robert J. "Federation for NRA." *Guns in American Society: An Encyclopedia of History, Politics, Culture, and the Law, 2nd Edition.* 2012.

11. Harlan Carter: The New York Times, "Hard-Line Opponent of Gun Laws Wins New Term at Helm of Rifle." May 4, 1981. http://www.nytimes.com/1981/05/04/us/hard-line-opponent-of-gun-laws-wins-new-term-at-helm-of-rifle.html

*Ch. 13:*

1. 1972 Republican party platform: Moyers and Company, "The Rise of the NRA." June 12, 2014. http://billmoyers.com/2014/06/12/the-rise-of-the-nra-2/

2. *fine with gun control*: The New York Times, "Why I'm for the Brady Bill." Mar. 29, 1991. http://www.nytimes.com/1991/03/29/opinion/why-i-m-for-the-brady-bill.html

3. tens of millions of dollars: Center for Responsive Politics, "National Rifle Association – Profile for 2016 Election Cycle." https://www.opensecrets.org/orgs/summary.php?id=d000000082

4. unarmed black teenagers: New York Times, "After Florida Shooting, NRA Crowd Sticks to What it Knows." Apr. 15, 2012.

5. recall elections: The New York Times, "Colorado Lawmakers Ousted in Recall Vote Over Gun Law." Sept. 11, 2013. http://www.nytimes.com/2013/09/11/us/colorado-lawmaker-concedes-defeat-in-recall-over-gun-law.html?_r=0

6. Fights background checks: Portland Press Herald, "NRA Official Urges Mainers to Reject Background Checks on Gun Sales." Aug. 24, 2016. http://www.pressherald.com/2016/08/24/nra-official-urges-mainers-to-reject-background-checks-on-gun-sales/

7. waiting periods: The Trace, "The NRA is Taking Credit for the Background Check System It Tried to Sink." Jan. 12. 2016. https://www.thetrace.org/2016/01/nra-background-check-system-brady-bill-wayne-lapierre/

8. safe storage laws: Nashville Scene, "NRA Disregards Kids' Safety Law, Shoots Down MaKayla's Law." Mar. 2, 2016. http://www.nashvillescene.com/news/pith-in-the-wind/article/13063356/nra-disregards-kids-safety-shoots-down-makaylas-law

9. Surgeon General appointee: The Huffington Post, Senate Confirms Vivek Murthy as Surgeon General over Republican Opposition." Dec. 16, 2014. http://www.huffingtonpost.com/2014/12/15/surgeon-general-vote_n_6329884.html

10. weaken gun laws: Politifact, "A Summary of the Manchin-Toomey Gun Proposal." Apr. 30, 2013. http://www.politifact.com/truth-o-meter/article/2013/apr/30/summary-manchin-toomey-gun-proposal/

11. "Stand Your Ground": Social Science and Medicine, "Race, law, and health: Examination of 'Stand Your Ground' and defendant convictions in Florida." Oct. 2015, 194-201. http://www.sciencedirect.com/science/article/pii/S0277953615300642

12. cranks out lies: LiveScience, "Guns Don't Deter Crime, Study Finds." July 6, 2015. http://www.livescience.com/51446-guns-do-not-deter-crime.html

13. over $300 million a year: The Trace, "New NRA Tax Filing Shows Membership Revenues Dropped by $47 Million Following Sandy Hook Surge." Jan. 23, 2016. https://www.thetrace.org/2016/01/new-nra-tax-filing-shows-membership-revenues-dropped-by-47-million-following-sandy-hook-surge/

14. Tax-free: NRA Foundation, "Notice Regarding Declaration of Nonprofit Status." 2016. https://www.nrafoundation.org/grants/notice-regarding-documentation-of-nonprofit-status/

15. here: The Washington Post, "Has Your U.S. Congress Person Received Donations from the NRA?" June 21, 2016. https://www.washingtonpost.com/graphics/national/nra-donations/

16. Dickey Amendment: PUBLIC LAW 104–208—SEPT. 30, 1996. https://www.gpo.gov/fdsys/pkg/PLAW-104publ208/pdf/PLAW-104publ208.pdf\

17. deep regrets: NPR, "Ex-Rep Dickey Regrets Restrictive Law on Gun Violence Research." Oct. 9, 2015. http://www.npr.org/2015/10/09/447098666/ex-rep-dickey-regrets-restrictive-law-on-gun-violence-research

18. fought the Brady bill: The Trace, "How America Wound up with a Gun Background Check System Built More for Speed than Certainty." July 21, 2015. https://www.thetrace.org/2015/07/brady-bill-amendment-default-proceed-loophole-amendment-nra/

19. takes credit: The Trace, "The NRA Is Taking Credit for the Background Check System it Tried to Sink." Jan. 12, 2016. https://www.thetrace.org/2016/01/nra-background-check-system-brady-bill-wayne-lapierre/

20. armor-piercing: Bloomberg, "What You Need to Know About the Armor-Piercing Bullet Controversy." Mar. 12, 2015. http://www.bloomberg.com/news/articles/2015-03-12/what-you-need-to-know-about-the-armor-piercing-bullet-controversy

21. PLCAA: Public Law 109-92 109th Congress.

22. forced to pay gun manufacturers' legal fees: The Washington Free Beacon, "Federal Judge Orders Plaintiffs to Pay Ammo Dealer's Legal Fees After Dismissing Lawsuit." June 29, 2015. http://freebeacon.com/issues/federal-judge-orders-brady-center-to-pay-ammo-dealers-legal-fees-after-dismissing-lawsuit/

23. irresponsibly: Illinois Review, "Baseball, Apple Pie and AR-15 – 'Pure American' Chicago Billboard Says." Jan, 26, 2014. http://illinoisreview.typepad.com/illinoisreview/2014/01/baseball-apple-pie-and-ar-15-pure-american-chicago-billboard-says.html

24. they're already here: Smart Tech Challenges Foundation, "News and Updates." 2016. https://smarttechfoundation.org/smart-gun-news-and-updates/

25. trigger locks and safes: FOX 13 Salt Lake City, "Utah Company Making Guns Safer with Fingerprint Trigger Lock." Jan, 6, 2016. http://fox13now.com/2016/01/06/wvc-company-makes-guns-safe-with-fingerprint-trigger-lock/

26. <u>failure rate</u>: Media Matters for American, "What to Know About the NRA and Smart Guns." Apr. 29, 2016. http://mediamatters.org/research/2016/04/29/what-know-about-nra-and-smart-guns/210147

27. <u>no other testing laboratory</u>: National Institute of Justice Research Report: A Review of Gun Safety Technologies. June 2013. https://www.ncjrs.gov/pdffiles1/nij/242500.pdf

28. <u>one percent</u>: MSNBC, "The Smart Gun Fight Rages On." May 6, 2014. http://www.msnbc.com/all-in/watch/the-smart-gun-fight-rages-on-248687171857

29. <u>turn your gun on or off</u>: American Rifleman, "Smart Guns: Dude, You Hacked My Gun." Apr. 25, 2014. https://www.americanrifleman.org/articles/2014/4/25/smart-guns-dude-you-hacked-my-gun/

30. <u>threats and attacks</u>: Reuters, "Maryland Gun Store Drops Plans to Sell 'Smart Guns' After Threats." May 2, 2014. http://www.reuters.com/article/us-usa-maryland-smartgun-idUSBREA410SD20140502

31. <u>scared to sell them</u>: Mother Jones, "The Guns the NRA Doesn't Want You to Get." Nov. 3, 2015.

32. <u>opposition to smart guns</u>: NRA-ILA, "'Smart' Guns: Personalized Firearms." 2016. https://www.nraila.org/issues/smart-gunspersonalized-firearms/

33. gun sales skyrocket: New York Times, "What Happens After Calls for New Gun Restrictions? Sales Go Up." June 13, 2016. http://www.nytimes.com/interactive/2015/12/10/us/gun-sales-terrorism-obama-restrictions.html?_r=0

*Ch. 14:*

1. faking his research: Mother Jones, "Double Barreled Double Standards." Oct. 13, 2003. http://www.motherjones.com/politics/2003/10/double-barreled-double-standards

2. "the Bible of the gun lobby": Weiner, Jon. "John Lott, Gun Rights, and Research Fraud." *Historians in Trouble: Plagiarism, Fraud, and Politics in the Ivory Tower*. New York: The New Press, 2004. https://books.google.com/books?id=rYY7AAAAQBAJ&pg=PA136#v=onepage&q&f=false

3. escalate to violence: Psychology Today, "The 'Weapons Effect.'" Jan. 18, 2013. https://www.psychologytoday.com/blog/get-psyched/201301/the-weapons-effect

4. Gary Kleck: Crime Prevention Research Center, 'CPRC's John Lott Continued Debate with Gary Kleck over his attacks on 'More Guns, Less Crime.'" Dec. 24, 2015. http://crimeresearch.org/2015/12/cprcs-john-lott-continued-debate-with-gary-kleck-over-more-guns-less-crime/

5. a single telephone survey: Armed with Reason, "Defensive Gun Use: Gary Kleck Misfires Again." Mar. 9, 2015. http://www.armedwithreason.com/defensive-gun-use-gary-kleck-misfires-again/

6. 11,622 gun homicides: National Vital Statistics Reports, "Deaths: Final Data for 2012." Aug. 23, 2015. http://www.cdc.gov/nchs/data/nvsr/nvsr63/nvsr63_09.pdf

7. justifiable self-defense: Violence Policy Center, "Firearm Justifiable Homicides and Non-Fatal Self-Defense Gun Use." June 2015. http://www.vpc.org/studies/justifiable15.pdf

8. methodology: Journal of Political Economy, "More Guns, More Crime." Vol. 5, no. 5, 2001. http://www.kellogg.northwestern.edu/faculty/dranove/htm/Dranove/coursepages/Mgmt%20469/guns.pdf

9. sock puppet persona: Reason.com, "The Mystery of Mary Rosh." May 2003. http://reason.com/archives/2003/05/01/the-mystery-of-mary-rosh

10. under the names of his colleagues: Plassman and Whitby's Statement on the Stanford Law Review Debate. June 9, 2003. http://johnrlott.tripod.com/postsbyday/6-9-03.html

11. Arthur Kellermann: Guns and Crime, "Increased Civilian Gun Ownership Will Not Reduce Crime." 2015. http://tinyurl.com/j5ddhl3

12. Researchers at Harvard: Harvard Injury Control Research Center, "Homicides." https://www.hsph.harvard.edu/hicrc/firearms-research/guns-and-death/

13. willingness to deceive: Townhall, "The Other Lott Controversy." Feb. 5, 2003. http://townhall.com/columnists/michellemalkin/2003/02/05/the_other_lott_controversy

14. Fred Rivara: Salon, "The Answer is Not More Guns." Dec. 17, 2012. http://www.salon.com/2012/12/18/the_answer_is_not_more_guns/

15. details every single methodological flaw: Armed with Reason, "Shooting Down the Gun Lobby's Favorite 'Academic': A Lott of Lies." Dec. 1, 2014. http://sph.washington.edu/faculty/fac_bio.asp?url_ID=Rivara_Frederick

16. omitting tables: ScienceBlogs, "Lott Tries to Rewrite History, Again." Feb. 27, 2004. http://scienceblogs.com/deltoid/2004/02/27/johnlottorg/

17. the entire state of Florida: Journal of Legal Studies, "Do Right-to-Carry Laws Deter Violent Crime?" Vol. 27, no. 1, Jan. 1998. http://www.journals.uchicago.edu/doi/10.1086/468019

18. online content: Deltoid, "Lott Puts the 'Con' into 'Economics.'" Sept. 11, 2003. http://web.archive.org/web/20050616121221/http:/timlambert.org/2003/09/0910/

19. reasonable doubt: The Los Angeles Times, "Shooting Holes in a Lawsuit." May 31, 2006. http://articles.latimes.com/2006/may/31/opinion/oe-wiener31

20. Daniel Webster: The Washington Post, "More Guns, Less Crime? Not Exactly." July 29, 2014. https://www.washingtonpost.com/news/wonk/wp/2014/07/

21. aggravated assaults: Johns Hopkins Bloomberg School of Public Health, "The Case for Gun Policy Reforms in America." 9. https://web.archive.org/web/20130307065951/http:/www.jhsph.edu/research/centers-and-institutes/johns-hopkins-center-for-gun-policy-and-research/publications/WhitePaper102512_CGPR.pdf#page=9

22. American Law and Economics Review: "The Impact of Right-to-Carry Laws and the NRC Report: Lessons for the Empirical Evaluation of Law and Policy." 2011. https://works.bepress.com/john_donohue/89/

23. decreases or increases: The National Academies Press, "Firearms and Violence: A Critical Review." 2004. https://www.nap.edu/read/10881/chapter/2

24. can understand, let alone refute: The Skeptical Inquirer, "Myths of Murder and Multiple Regression." Vol. 26, no. 1, January/February 2002. 19-23. http://www.crab.rutgers.edu/~goertzel/mythsofmurder.htm

## Ch. 15:

1. 83 mass shootings: Mother Jones, "A Guide to Mass Shootings in America." Sept. 24, 2016. http://www.motherjones.com/politics/2012/07/mass-shootings-map

2. one-half and two-thirds: Mother Jones, "Maybe What We Need is a Better Mental Health Policy." Nov. 9, 2012. http://www.motherjones.com/politics/2012/11/jared-loughner-mass-shootings-mental-illness

3. law enforcement and/or military: Mother Jones, "Do Armed Civilians Stop Mass Shootings? Actually, No." Dec. 19, 2012. http://www.motherjones.com/politics/2012/12/armed-civilians-do-not-stop-mass-shootings

4. Would-be Good Guys: BBC News, "Las Vegas 'Good Guy with a Gun' – Victim or Martyr?" June 17, 2014. http://www.bbc.com/news/blogs-echochambers-27892820

5. ending up dead: Tyler Morning Telegraph, "Survivors Remember Deadly Downtown Tyler Gun Battle." Feb. 24, 2015. http://www.tylerpaper.com/TP-News%20Local/214462/survivors-remember-deadly-downtown-tyler-gun-battle

6. just might: Slate, "Friendly Firearms." Jan. 11, 2011. http://www.slate.com/articles/health_and_science/human_nature/2011/01/friendly_firearms.html

7. make their job harder: Los Angeles Times, "Dallas Police Chief: Open Carry Makes Things Confusing During Mass Shootings." July 11, 2016. http://www.latimes.com/nation/la-na-dallas-chief-20160711-snap-story.html

8. Colin Goddard: InMaricopa.com, "Virginia Tech Shooting Survivor: Guns on Campus Won't Save Lives." Mar. 3, 2011. http://www.inmaricopa.com/virginia-tech-shooting-survivor-guns-on-campus-wont-save-lives/

9. estimates: New Republic, "Here's Why No One Can Agree on the Number of Mass Shootings." Oct. 3, 2015. https://newrepublic.com/article/123027/heres-why-no-one-can-agree-number-mass-shootings

10. definitions: The Washington Post, "We Have Three Different Definitions of 'Mass Shooting,' and We Probably Need More." Feb. 26, 2016. https://www.washingtonpost.com/news/wonk/wp/2016/02/26/we-have-three-different-definitions-of-mass-shooting-and-we-probably-need-more/

11. grand total of 5: FBI.gov, "FBI Releases Study on Active Shooter Incidents." Sept. 24, 2014. https://www.fbi.gov/news/stories/fbi-releases-study-on-active-shooter-incidents

12. 4 or more fatalities: FBI.gov, "Serial Murder: Multi-Disciplinary Perspectives for Investigators." https://www.fbi.gov/stats-services/publications/serial-murder#two

13. map: Gun Violence Archive, 2016. http://www.gunviolencearchive.org/

14. too many to keep accurate track of: Time Magazine, "34 Years of Mass Shootings in One Chart." June 14, 2016. http://time.com/4368615/orlando-mass-shootings-chart/

15. on the rise: Mother Jones, "Rate of Mass Shootings Has Tripled Since 2011, Harvard Research Shows." Oct. 15, 2014. http://www.motherjones.com/politics/2014/10/mass-shootings-increasing-harvard-research

*Ch. 16:*

1. roll back many of these laws: Fordham Law Review, "On Gun Registration, the NRA, Adolf Hitler, and Nazi Gun Laws: Exploding the Gun Culture Wars (A Call to Historians)." Vol. 73 #2, 2004. http://ir.lawnet.fordham.edu/cgi/viewcontent.cgi?article=4029&context=flr

2. passing tighter gun control laws: Los Angeles Times, "After Its Own Mass Shootings, Germany Beefed Up Gun Control Laws. The Number of Shootings Dropped." June 15, 2016. http://www.latimes.com/world/europe/la-fg-germany-gun-control-20160615-snap-story.html

3. many Jews possessed guns: Politifact, "Fact-Checking Ben Carson's Claim That Gun Control Laws Allowed Nazis to Carry Out Holocaust." Oct. 26, 2015. http://www.politifact.com/truth-o-meter/statements/2015/oct/26/ben-carson/fact-checking-ben-carson-nazi-guns/

4. NRA board member: NRA on the Record, "Member Profile: Ted Nugent." http://nraontherecord.org/ted-nugent/

*Ch. 17:*

1. toxic masculinity: Aeon, "The Weaponized Loser." 2016. https://aeon.co/essays/humiliation-and-rage-how-toxic-masculinity-fuels-mass-shootings

2. evidence: Econbrowser, "Mass Shooting Casualties, by Religion of Perpetrator: Muslim vs. Non-Muslim." June 12, 2016. http://econbrowser.com/archives/2015/12/mass-shooting-casualties-by-religion-of-perpetrator-muslim-vs-non-muslim

3. violent jihadist attacks: New America, "America's Layered Defenses." 2016. http://www.newamerica.org/in-depth/terrorism-in-america/what-threat-united-states-today/#americas-layered-defenses

4. as investigators do: NPR, "Investigators Say Orlando Shooter Showed Few Warning Signs of Radicalization." June 18, 2016. http://www.npr.org/sections/thetwo-way/2016/06/18/482621690/investigators-say-orlando-shooter-showed-few-warning-signs-of-radicalization

5. true: National Institute of Justice, "Gun Violence." Apr. 4, 2013. http://www.nij.gov/topics/crime/gun-violence/pages/welcome.aspx

6. no meaningful correlation: Massachusetts General Hospital, "Research Shows Violent Media Do Not Cause Violent Behavior." Dec. 26, 2012. http://www.massgeneral.org/psychiatry/news/newsarticle.aspx?id=3929

7. six gun deaths: GunPolicy.org, "Japan: Gun Facts, Figures and the Law." 2016. http://www.gunpolicy.org/firearms/region/japan

8. other 95% of shootings: Everytown Research Center, "Analysis of Mass Shootings." 2015. https://everytownresearch.org/reports/mass-shootings-analysis/

9. mental illness: American Journal of Public Health, "Mental Illness, Mass Shootings, and the Politics of American Firearms." Vol. 105 no. 2, Feb. 2015. 240-49. https://www.ncbi.nlm.nih.gov/pmc/articles/PMC4318286/

10. insanely easy access to guns: The Trace, "Watch an Al-Quaeda Spokesman Talk About How Easy It Is to Buy Guns in the U.S." Nov. 18, 2015. https://www.thetrace.org/2015/11/islamic-extremists-gun-sale-loopholes/

*Ch. 18:*

1. <u>by a wide margin</u>: Center for American Progress, "Gun Owners Overwhelmingly Support Background Checks, See NRA as Out of Touch, New Poll Finds." Nov. 17, 2015. https://www.americanprogress.org/press/release/2015/11/17/125618/release-gun-owners-overwhelmingly-support-background-checks-see-nra-as-out-of-touch-new-poll-finds/

2. <u>stopped representing them</u>: The Washington Post, "Most Gun Owners Don't Belong to the NRA – and They Don't Agree with It, Either." Oct. 15, 2015. https://www.washingtonpost.com/news/wonk/wp/2015/10/15/most-gun-owners-dont-belong-to-the-nra-and-they-dont-agree-with-it-either/

Printed in Great Britain
by Amazon